LUC

LANDING PAGE EFFECTIVENESS

CONQUER THE MARKET WITH AN INVINCIBLE OFFER

Boost your sales and contacts from the web using the best response to your customer's problems

Copyright © 2016 Luca Orlandini
Futura Inmagine SL
Calle La Gomera 1, 35660 Corralejo (Las Palmas)
Tel. +39 3294534340 –
e-mail sl@futuraimmagine.com

www.landing-page-effectiveness.com

No part of this book may be reproduced, incorporeted into computer system or transmitted in any for or by any means, electronic, mechanical, photocopying, recording or otherwise, without the prior writte permission of the author.
Infringement of the above-mentioned rights may contitute a crime.

Cover: Luca Orlandini

Editing: Michela Bresaz

To Alessia for all your help, support and advice.
Without you none of this would have been possible.

INDEX

PREFACE BY FRANCESCO TINTI   XV

Keep your feet on the ground   1

About Me   3

The Invincible Offering   5
What you won't find in this book   5
What you will find in this book   6
Our objective   7
Why must you only focus on what is important?   7

The landing page   13
How does it work?   13
Costs, truths and priorities   15
How does an effective lead generation system work?   18

Rising above Google   21
Why can't being first be the primary objective?   25
Why is a landing page a crucial instrument?   26

VIII | Contents

The importance of strategy — 29

TODAY THE WINNER IS YOU: AIDA REVISED — 33
The additional elements — 34
The problem (or the need) — 34
Trust — 35
Extended satisfaction (and the surprise) — 36
Feedback — 36
The funnel's efficiency — 37
Today the winner is you – an easy way to remember a method — 37

Part 1 – The landing phase — 41
TODAY

Introduction
Building rapport happens in small steps — 43

CHAPTER 1

Identify the problem — 47
Defining the service's target — 53

CHAPTER 2
The rules of attraction
Images — 62
    A. An image that reflects the product's benefit — 63

B. The importance of emotion	65
C. Representing the professional service provider	67
When is it best to include a photo?	69
Images must explain and highlight the text	70
If the photo is of a person, it should look at the CTA	73
How to test if an image is suitable	75
Above the fold copywriting	76
The Unique Selling Proposition	79
How to write an offering's headline	82
Testing and improving above the fold copy	86
Optimising attention	87
Visuals must not prevaricate on copy	88
Making the Call To Action (CTA) clear	92
Is it true that landing pages must not have a navigation menu?	97
How to test the above the fold's attention	98

CHAPTER 3
The rules of interest — 101

Avoiding WYSIATI	102
The presentation video	103
Incontrovertible truths	106
Progressive Information	109
How to make on-screen text more legible	113
First anchor	120

Part 2 — The conversion phase — 125
THE WINNER

Introduction — 127
Having obtained trust, now you must close the sale — 127

Chapter 4
Forging trust — 129
Client references — 130
    How must references be laid out? — 132
    Reference text and credibility — 133
    Client reviews that aren't only positive — 139
    How many references to publish and where — 141
The money back guarantee — 142
The "free" trial — 146
    Resist temptation from the dark side, use
       the default option wisely — 150

Chapter 5
The rules of desire — 157
How to use bait (and connect the anchor) — 158
    Why too many choices are a problem — 163
    Helping a choice to be made through social proof — 165
    Listing prices according to the contrast principle — 167
Urgency and avversion to missed opportunity — 168
    A. Limited time offer — 169
    B. Limiting the number of pieces available — 173
    C. Limiting quantity according to price — 176
Desire after action

Chapter 6
The rules of action — 181

Lead optimisation and downsell	182
When you ask too much: downsell	185
Simplify and facilitate contact	188
7 usability rules for forms of contact	192
7 usability rules for contact forms	194
Get more! Upsell	195

Part 3 – The satisfaction phase
IS YOU
Introduction   209

The subtle difference between getting clients and creating an outstanding business   209

CHAPTER 7
Extended satisfaction   213

CHAPTER 8
Obtain references   221

Useful feedback and useless feedback	223
A. Fake feedback	223
B. Real feedback that isn't too credible	224
C. Real feedback the user doesn't identify with	225
D. Real feedback that is lacking in content	225
How to begin	227
Put yourself to the test right away!	231

CHAPTER 9

Make the funnel efficient — 233
Efficiency in acquisition — 235
Efficiency in lead management — 239
    How to take full advantage of user with remarketing — 239
    How to obtain conversions thanks to lead nurturing — 241
Increasing customer life-time value — 243

Part 4 – In-depth information — 249

From landing page effectiveness to Invincible Offer — 251

Profiled traffic — 253
The importance of brand positioning — 254
Your fantastic surprises — 257

Brand positioning — 259
Does a fundamental element for business success exist? — 259
    TEST: Is there a basis for your business? — 260
    This is what brand positioning is for — 261
    Small businesses' misunderstanding about marketing — 262
    If you're not big, you must be precise — 262
    Rule n° 1 of brand positioning:
    "Use your mind stairs" — 263
    Rule n° 2 of brand positioning:
    "You must be different, not the best" — 267
    Rule n° 3 of brand positioning:
    "Always and only communicate your brand positioning" — 271
A last piece of advice — 275

Contents | XIII

Targeted profile — **277**
Does a fundamental element for business success exist? — 277
    The purchasing funnel: how people buy products and services — 279
    Identifying the target audience — 281
Google AdWords versus Facebook Ads — 282

Almost all the images in this book are taken from the
author's work in the Italian market.
To increase understanding of the text,
we've tried to translate its pages into English,
trying to preserve the meaning of the words.

PREFACE
BY FRANCESCO TINTI

What you are about to read is a guide to the development of high impact landing pages and sales offerings. Unlike a standard web page, a landing page is carefully structured and designed in its every detail in order to achieve one objective: convince the user to act immediately and get a result. We work in the field of direct response marketing, the kind of marketing that not only makes a message memorable – just like traditional advertising does – but also brings about a response to the stimulus received (hence the name "direct response" marketing).

It's a kind of marketing that can be described as "scientific" in that nothing is left to chance and it uses a scientific method that makes the effects of every single action measurable.

The fundamental elements of direct response marketing are:
1. convincing the user;
2. inviting the user to act immediately;
3. measuring the results.

As you can see these elements are simple, extremely practical and most of all not new. At a time when social media marketing, content marketing and youdecidethename-marketing are all we hear about, I realise how very often we loose touch with the fundamental reason for doing marketing: to identify a problem being experienced by a target audience and then offer a uniquely positioned solution to the market. With respect to this, direct response marketing is incredibly concrete and it is perfect for the web in that it allows for the scientific measurement of results.

As mentioned, the concepts are not new because direct response marketing has existed for over a hundred years, time during which it has gone through three phases of development. It was born in the United States towards the end of the 19th century and in 1923 its principles were first set-out by

Claude C. Hopkins in "Scientific Advertising", an extraordinary publication that is a must-read for every marketer, salesman and advertiser.

Of course in Hopkins' day there was no internet or television. Starting in 1919 radio programmes began spreading but the main means of advertising was still print. It was in the newspapers and magazines of the time that advertorials and sales letters, the predecessors of the modern-day landing page, were first published.

The next phase consisted in the transition from the newspaper to the mailbox, from the article to the personally addressed letter. While the means changed, the structure of the sales letter was well defined and its results measurable.

Think of the letters you receive in your mailbox from nonprofit organisations every year towards November and December, asking for donations for cancer research, long-distance adoption or the homeless. Yes, these are printed landing pages.

The third and last phase of direct response marketing is on the web, where it has taken the shape of the landing page and its derivatives the squeeze page and the optin page.

In the book you are about to read, Luca Orlandini introduces you to landing pages and the steps to building them, the result of over ten thousand hours of work in the field.

Luca has "modeled" the best successful case studies from which he has defined a framework and taken the key elements that must always be present in a truly invincible landing page. However, Luca had gone much further than this.

He has found his own very personal style that turns a generic landing page into a "Invincible Offering" landing page. First and foremost is the symbiosis between presentation and content, because for Luca an aesthetically pleasing landing page will always be better at converting users to clients compared to an ugly landing page with the same content.

As well as citing numerous authors, Luca uses real cases to explain how he has applied more and lesser known principles of persuasion that Cialdini, Ariely and other world renowned experts defined long ago.

Luca has deconstructed and extracted the main parts and rules that he believes make the difference and guarantee a landing page's success: problem, attraction, interest, trust, desire, action, satisfaction.

Between the lines Luca also tells us of his experiences as a web marketing consultant and a serial developer of landing pages, describing episodes, curiosities and anecdotes from his everyday work. Understanding these as you read the book is fundamental for you too.

Francesco Tinti

KEEP YOUR FEET ON THE GROUND

Reading this book won't be enough to make you a landing page expert.
I realise this might not be the most commercially sound way to start the book and I hope the publisher will forgive me, however I firmly believe that one of the main jobs of an author preparing educational content is to make sure his or her readers have realistic expectations.

I want to write it here as a premise, in order for it to be clear from the get-go.

Every day I read of magical methods, sneaky tricks and miraculous techniques that generate clients from nothing. All you apparently have to do is find a good Wi-Fi network and then watch your bank account grow while sipping a cocktail on a sandy beach.

Unfortunately this isn't the way things work in real life and I define these as "scratchcard jackpot" approaches.
A lottery ticket buyer doesn't really believe he will become rich. He knows well that he would have a far greater chance of winning by betting on red or black in a game of roulette, but then again he isn't interested in probability. What he is buying is the dream, the possibility of changing his life from one moment to the next. He is buying that pleasing feeling that accompanies hope and that persists from when he hands over his money to when he has scratched his card to realise that yet again this wasn't his lucky day.

Despite this being a large and steadily growing market, this book is not for those who have the above described objective. Life doesn't change from

2 Keep your feet on the ground

one moment to the next, it doesn't do so automatically and generally it doesn't do so while you have your feet buried in the sand. Life changes while you work, study and make mistakes. Life changes as you gather experience.

It's experience that makes you an expert.

Finding the best resources to study and the methods that work certainly isn't easy. It is the details that may appear to be unimportant that actually have a decisive impact on results.

This is precisely what I am offering to you in this book: a summary of about ten thousand hours of specific experience in building effective landing pages that work, so that you may obtain results faster than I did.

Hopefully also making fewer mistakes.

How good you will become mainly depends on you: my job is simply to show you the best route, the one I know and travel on every day.

Just like a car, a process for online client acquisition is an instrument that is at first hard to control properly. Think how hard it was to apply the right amount of pressure to the clutch when you began driving. With the correct instructions and a suitable person by your side, learning will be easier and more gratifying. The sooner you get into the learning mindset, the sooner we can enjoy our journey together.

So, shall we begin?

In order for you to see the images of the book in colour, read further information and obtain free updates, we have setup the following support website

Https://landing-page-effectiveness.com/gym/

ABOUT ME

Hi, my name is Luca Orlandini and I am a marketing consultant specialised in the acquisition of new online clients. I have over 10,200 hours of experience specifically in the development of web pages meant to generate sales.

Many years ago I had the good fortune to read "Influence" by Robert Cialdini and to be completely intrigued by it. Many other excellent books followed and over time my way of working changed radically.

Today my job consists in improving the offering of companies by adapting them for the web to increase the chances that a website visit will result in a purchase, a quotation or a contact for my client. I use scientific advertising techniques that I combine creatively with notions of cognitive psychology to create tireless means of sale that display your offering 24 hours a day and also generate contact requests.

My understanding of the reasons behind user behaviour allows me to design web pages that obtain better results and therefore pursue my mission: to develop "Invincible Offerings" capable of changing the dynamics of a market niche.

I study and read books in Italian, English and Spanish that deal with advertising, marketing and sales because experience (my own and that of others doing my same job) is a key factor in reducing risk and creating effective communication from the outset.

Without experience we'd be reduced to merely using good practice and intuition. We would not be able to take full advantage of the knowledge that has over the years has come to be known as communication science, thanks to Hopkins and others who have believed in hard selling.
However there is a vast sea of educational material regarding sales, copy and psycology in which it is easy to flounder, loosing all sense of direction;

4 Who I am

this is why I must thank Francesco Tinti (my mentor in many disciplines), Rossella Cenini, Enrico Madrigrano, Marco De Veglia, Filippo Toso, Giulio Marsala. Studying your work, as well as having the opportunity to exchange thoughts with you, has been more valuable than reading any book and more revealing than any A/B test.

A huge thanks also goes to experts such as Neil Patel, Oli Gardner, Peep Laja, Micheal Aagaard, Sean D'Souza, Angie Schottmuller and all those who study user behaviour to then openly share their findings.

In this book I will do my utmost to summarise the tactics I have learnt and the strategies I use every day. I will do this by describing real cases and giving a step by step explanation of my personal method for reaching the one objective that everybody attributes value to: selling.

A number of friends have asked me why I've decided to share knowledge that I have developed over many years of relentless study, revealing what has more often than not proven to be a winning hand. It's really quite simple: by explaining these concepts I give them a clear stucture in my mind, with further continuous study becoming the natural consequence.

Let's be clear, these are not techniques that have turned me into a millionaire, but they've allowed me to effectively promote and grow my business, giving me and my family the security needed to lead a happy and fulfilling life. I believe that this is the only thing that truly matters.

While you learn the strategies that have already proven to be effective in my case, I will be working on new methods and projects. I hope that in future editions I will have the chance to share these too :).

THE INVINCIBLE OFFERING

Congratulations for buying the strategic manual for the creation of an effective landing page that will help you win market share, it's great to come into the life of those who want to improve their results.

If you've bought this book you are in all likelihood looking to:
- Understand how to increase sales or requests for quotes from your web pages;
- Acquire a strategic method that will allow you be successful in the long-term.

Whichever of these is your objective, in these pages you will find all the experience that I have matured to date, organised into a step by step itinerary that will use real examples and cases I have faced to guide you from start to finish.

You will discover my method for obtaining results. I have engagingly called it "Today the winner is you" and I will show you how to apply it to your online business, whatever it might be.

Most importantly of all you will understand which activities you should pay greater attention to and what the essential steps for market success are, whether online or offline.

What you won't find in this book

This book is a strategic manual aimed at entrepreneurs or consultants who want to understand how to structure their offering in order to get more results.

It is not a technical manual that explains how to build your own website or how to configure WordPress or Joomla!. You will not find code or PHP but the clear and simple language used will help you understand how to correctly manage and direct your staff.

If you are an entrepreneur YOU CANNOT build your own effective website with this or other manuals.

You must begin with a different objective: figure out what strategy you plan to follow, what you will ask technicians to implement and how best to spend your money to get the results you need.

What you will find in this book

This is a step by step guide to your users decision making process, from the moment in which your user manifests a need or a problem that your offering represents a solution for, to when he or she clicks on your contact form's send button.

More than half of our itinerary will relate to developing the offering and creating an effective landing page, i.e. the ideal destination where to direct all those who are interested in your ads.

However we won't be stopping here. In the third part of the manual we will understand how to best meet your client's expectations and make the offering even better thanks to his feedback. Lastly we will implement strategies to optimise the cost of acquisition, thereby creating the perfect sales funnel.

> Note
>
> I am not promising you a system that automatically generates clients without needing you to do anything, as unfortunately this doesn't exist. Great effort, hard work and investment are necessary to get results. What I can promise you is that once you put this book down to begin creating your offering, all your efforts will be focused on the essential activities that really make a difference when it comes to online success.

Our objective

We will put together an offering that will be the best possible solution to a specific market need. People searching the web for information will be attracted to our ads and will come to see our offer.

By reducing risk for users to a minimum and motivating them thanks to powerful leverage that uses emotions and psychology, we will convince them to not postpone any action and immediately make a purchase or contact us.

Our service will satisfy users above their expectations, so much so that it will generate word of mouth.

We will collect persuasive references that, once published, will increase the effectiveness of our page.

Furthemore, following the first sale we will plan successive sales, increasing the value of the client over time and building a relationship based on trust. Only at this point will we concentrate on organic trafic by implementing processes that will allow us to reduce acquisition costs even further.

Why must you only focus on what is important?

I've always been passionate about optimisation: since I began working in marketing over fifteen years ago, I have always tried to find ways to obtain the maximum result with minimum effort.

However it isn't always that easy.

When I started freelancing I was working far more than I do now, I was more stressed and I was getting less results. Often I would waste time pursuing late paying clients while my work flow resembled tropical rainfall.

I would have just a few projects for months to then suddenly end up working

8 | The unbeatable offer

18 hour days for weeks. When working this way I had no concern for costs. Taxation killed about 50% of my job so when I had any desire inherent in the work sphere I didn't think twice.

Although I thoroughly enjoyed what I was doing, my private life certainly wasn't benefiting from the stress caused by this pace of work. Despite my managing to earn enough to keep things afloat, considering my standard of living I was saving far too little.

Gradually I then began understanding.

The first step towards deliverance is not taking on every project by starting to say no.

No to who would commission a job to then think they could teach me what to do.

No to who would not agree to make a 50% down payment.

No to who, amicably or not, would treat me like a child and not as an equal simply because he was the client and I was the supplier. To be defined as such, a working relationship must be between two equals.

Initially I had a great deal of free time and I think I erroneously also said no to some very interesting projects.

However I could afford to do so.

I still had a mortgage to pay and I hadn't won the lottery, but I had changed the manner in which I related to my potential clients. While beforehand I had few requests so I had to accept them all, I now had far more requests than I could manage. So many in fact that I was being forced to refuse interesting projects too.

All of a sudden I realised that overdue invoices were no longer a problem. It had been months since worrying about late payments kept me up at night and years since I had issued a note of credit.

The unbeatable offer

At last, with far more requests than I could attend to, I was able to increase prices a little and dedicate more time to projects. I would stop working two hours earlier in the evenings and would use the extra time for my professional growth and study.

Finally I had the time to observe the market to understand how it would develop and then predict trends, putting me one step ahead of the competition.
Everything had fallen into place.

You are probably now thinking that a vital piece of the story is missing and you'd be right.

I told you that the number of requests increased, what I didn't tell you is how.
Put simply, I verticalised my capabilities and focused my communication on a specific and effective offering aimed at the small market niche I was interested in.

I began working on web projects in the 2,000 to 6,000 euro range, creating pre-defined package deals that I would customise together with the entrepreneur once purchased. The next step was to include landing pages in my package deals at a price of 1,300 euros.

I then adapted and streamlined further, offering landing pages at 1,500 euros and only accepting web projects in the 3,000 to 5,000 euro range, turning down projects that required programming or that were too structured in terms of their development. This way, with a higher budget, I could spend all the time needed on a project and also develop an effective communication strategy that went above and beyond what the client had in fact asked for.

I was selling websites, but they were effective websites with high conversion rates at below market price.

However, I needed to get more practice.

10 The unbeatable offer

Today, with over 10,200 hours of work on projects involving lead generation (client acquisition), I have a great deal of experience and I have clearly defined the method to structure any offering in the best way possible. I now work almost exclusively on the development of landing pages and the price of each project has more than doubled since I began.

The increase in price is not only the consequence of higher demand: it is the cause of it.

Having specialised in order to become the very best in just a few activities, I am now to a certain extent seen as a point of reference in my market niche. I've had the opportunity to choose the most interesting projects, dedicating 100% of my time only to aspects of communication that have a direct influence on sales.

All thanks to a specific offering.

About three years ago I left expensive Milan, that is too hot in summer and too cold in winter, in order to move to Fuerteventura in the Canary Islands with my wife Alessia and my cats Kiki and Diego. I consider our relocation to be proof of the fact that once you begin optimising your business and your life more generally, it's really difficult to then stop.

Quality of life always has repercussions on the quality of work: the temperate climate and getting organised have allowed me to be more productive while working less, to increase turnover and to reduce stress.

The extraordinary thing is that I feel as if I am only getting started and that I have a long way to go, but if I were to win the lottery tomorrow in all likelihood I would continue to live in exactly the same way as now.

If you like the idea and if you are also ready to optimise your business, we can start.

> **AUTHOR'S TIP**
>
> To get the most out of this book, I recommend that you don't read it when you are too tired, or above all, distracted.
>
> I recommend that you read slowly, maximum of one chapter at a time, to be able to take on board the concepts expressed and that you do the exercises that I propose at the end of each chapter.
>
> At the end of each of the three parts that comprise my method you will find a takeaway, that is, a brief summary of the most important concepts.
>
> On the support web page Https://landing-page-effectiveness.com/gym/, I have published all the images in colour and high resolution and also some other useful in-depth information that I advise you to read only when you have finished the book.
>
> Happy reading!

THE LANDING PAGE

The landing page is at the heart of our "Invincible Offer". It is an instrument of direct response marketing, a practice that has a measurable increase in sales, orders or information requests as its objective.

We can consider the landing page as the practical instrument through which the hard sell communication techniques developed throughout the last century are implemented.

"Hard sell" refers to a communication approach based on direct messages that are quick, simple and straightforward. This approach leads to an immediate response and has one objective: to sell a product or service.

During a period of recession it is fundamental that every effort be aimed at having direct repercussions on turnover. This is why direct response marketing is so successful. While large companies can afford to invest in advertising simply to increase brand recognition and awareness, smaller businesses need immediate, concrete and discernible results.

How does it work?

> People interested in a specific topic are intercepted and offered information (via video, e-book or articles) in exchange for their email address. There are no barriers to entry as the information is all free. What this does is establish a relational process (that can be more or less complex from an automation perspective) to engage the user until he or she is ready to make a purchase.
>
> Or:

14 | The Landing Page

> ▸ People who wish to find a solution to a specific need are intercepted and offered the best solution available. All possible objections to the user taking immediate action are removed. In this case barriers to entry are a little higher because the action needed requires a greater committment (phone contact, purchase, quotation request), however the final objective is of greater interest as it allows us to obtain the contact details of people ready to make a purchase.

Personally I choose the latter strategy or consider it preferable for two reasons:

- Firstly, if there are people in the market already willing to make a purchase, I don't see why I should focus on somebody who is not yet willing to do the same;
- Secondly, nothing stops me from focusing on this type of user once I have implemented a client acquisition system that brings about immediate results.

Think of woman whose car breaks down by the side of the road. She opens Google in order to look for help and finds a mechanic's advert. She then lands on the mechanic's website and instead of immediately having a number to call, she must first leave an email address and watch four videos before finally getting the mechanic's contact details.

Not exactly ideal, is it?

There are sure to be plenty of people interested in videos about car maintenance and avoiding breakdowns. I'm certain that by providing such content, at some stage users will end up being clients. However there are other priorities, especially if you are only at the start of your direct marketing experience.

You are probably thinking that my reasoning is perfectly logical and almost redundant. However there are dozens of entrepreneurs who, after having been "trained" by so-called coaches who over simplify the complex issues surrounding lead generation and online sales, end-up reasoning in the exact opposite way.

As you will have guessed the problem is not the instrument used: email marketing can be the cornerstone of your business, but if you are just starting out your priority is to respond to market demand in the most direct way possible.

The primary objective of our sales process will be to satisfy the requests of those who are close to making a purchase, so as to immediately generate sales and contacts.

After having reached this important result, meaning our business has truly become sustainable, we will also concentrate on who might be interested in purchasing our product but as a lead must first be informed or "warmed-up".

If you have therefore come to think of a landing page as a simple web page that promises something (a video, an e-book, a piece of miraculous advice) in exchange for your email, I must warn you that we will only be looking at this marginally and to the extent needed relative to our sales process.

Before reaching this point we will focus on creating a sales page capable of convincing your users that they need your product so that a direct contact to leading to a purchase is generated.

Costs, facts and priorities

The main problem I see in the market is that very often it's about what is possible and not what is necessary.

Let me better explain.

16 | The Landing Page

If you plan to open a physical shop and you receive a 40,000 $ quotation of the investment needed, you would never try to find the same solution for 2,000 $. You know perfectly well that it would make no sense and you'd never think "right, I'll buy some bricks and do it myself".

You must find 40,000 $ or otherwise you can try and find a 38,000 $ quotation, knowing full well that what you pay for is what you get. The exact opposite happens in the online world.

Why?

Entrepreneurs who should be defining and managing online business strategy or strategic marketing, are in actual fact dealing with operational maketing and therefore doing the job of technicians rather than their own. A number of problems derive from this: they don't pay attention to their main role, they waste large part of their investment and they loose faith in the online market.

If you are an entrepreneur, the first piece of advice that I can give you is to manage the strategy of your business, not the operational part. I work with the web and even I delegate some aspects such as PPC campaigns to technicians.

There are too many things to deal with and each of us can be prepared and truly competent in one thing only.

Every new additional notion that we decide to add to our remit takes time and resources from what our main activity should be. It deprives us of capability and experience in our job.

If you are an interior designer your main capability must be interior design, not the management of web marketing activities. You must keep up to date on new techniques, experiment with new colours and materials and get more practical experience so you can be the best in what you do.

However there is a problem: to understand your worth a potential client

The Landing Page 17

must first entrust you with their project. In order for this to happen you have to present your offering so that it is perceived as the best solution for the potential client's need or problem.

This is the reason why I created the Invincible Offer project. My objective will be to give you the benefit of all my experience in creating the content of your offering, one of three essential elements needed to be successful online and probably the most neglected and least known.

There are some very good guides on brand positioning and web traffic attraction, but these only superficially cover how to present an offering.

Some authors only reflect on copywriting, web design or user interfaces, while others only consider technical aspects in code implementation.
You are about to read a comprehensive and complete guide that will help you create an exceptional offering step by step.

I will not be teaching you techniques such as CSS or HTML language as the more we move forward the more you will come to realise these are only of secondary importance. Also, if you are an entrepreneur, learning about technicalities is not the best way to make use of your time.

It will be far more useful if instead you learn about the rules that differentiate a successful offering from an offering that is abbandoned within seconds. This is precisely what we are going to be doing in the next chapters.

Are you ready?

The Landing Page

How does an effective lead generation system work?

People are attracted to ads that promise to provide a solution to a specific problem and that link to a destination page where their "landing" is managed smoothly.
The most common definition of a landing page is as follows:

> *A landing page is a special page designed and created with the objective of motivating the user to take a specific action, also called a "conversion".*

The act of conversion can be the request for information, a subscription to a newspaper or the purchase of a product of service.

In reality, according to my experience and vision, a landing page should be more than a simple optimised page created with the objective of making the user carry out an action.

> *A landing page is a page that wants to give the best response to a person's needs creating an equal relationship of confidence and mutual benefit.*

Conversions are therefore the natural consequence of the relationship established between who has written the content and who is reading it.

Let's discuss this in more depth by understanding why we call it a landing page. The reason for calling it this way is that it is the perfect place for a person to "land" after having paid attention to an ad. In Spain, where people get straight to the point, it is called a "destination page". Of course being the destination of an ad doesn't qualify the page in terms of its results, so I prefer calling an optimised page an "effective" landing page.

There are many agencies online that that can design a landing page, but finding someone capable of developing one that is effecive isn't always easy.

The Landing Page

As you will find out in this guide, a few simple words can make a huge difference to results.

So why is having a user land here so useful?

The main reason is that we know precisely why the user has visited our page and we can make the conversion process more natural. As we said before, the landing page has ONE SINGLE OBJECTIVE. When a user visits a website's homepage we are still to understand why the visit is taking place and therefore there are many different kinds of content: there will be a link to services, to a blog, to references, to an about us section. The user's attention IS TOO THINLY SPREAD over a number of different things.

On the web just like with an airline flight, the landing (i.e. the moment in which the user first sees the page) is the most delicate stage. There is a risk that the user clicks back on the browser and that what was an opportunity turns into a cost.

While the impact of an aeroplane landing is given by its wheels hitting the ground, in our case it's a matter of the gap that there is between the user's expectations when clicking on the add and what he or she finds in the top part of the landing page.

To the greatest extent possible, all our communication must be natural and familiar to the user. On an effective landing page users will often skip the top part of the page entirely, scrolling downloads because the first thing they see is nothing more than confirmation of the content of the ad they clicked on. In the next, conversion focused stage, we will add information to reduce objections and encourage immediate action. Our objective will not only be to motivate the users to act, but more importantly still it will be to make them do so immediately, without postponing the decision.

Every time we are showing content to users we are in fact asking them to "invest" a little bit of their attention.

Creating an effective offering means generating as much value as possible from that small investment, with the user's dividend being the best solution available to his specific problem.

WHY YOU SHOULD BE ABOVE GOOGLE

> **What are we discussing here?**
> Everybody wants to be first in Google search results, but is it actually that important? Is an offering's online success completely dependant on Google?

I am returning home from my usual morning walk. It's 9.37 am on a Monday in January and the temperature is about 22°C. It looks like the start to a great day. Since moving to Fuerteventura I often wake up early enough to take a stroll before work. Walking helps me gather my thoughts, think through new project ideas and get some clarity on what the day's priorities are. As soon as I get home I sit at my desk while my cat Diego jumps onto my lap for his morning cuddle. Having switched on my Mac I open Pages to write another page of my book when an email catches my attention. "Another one", I dishearteningly think to myself after having read the first few lines. The prospective client and sender is called Marco.

22 | To be at the top of Google

"Dear Mr. Orlandini,
my name is Marco Bianchi of the Best gym.
I am contacting you after having heard you speak at the JoomlaDay convention in Florence a few weeks ago. I would like to ask you and FuturaImmagine to build my new company website.
We want to maximise our visibility on Google and on other search engines for as many keywords as possible and therefore may I ask you to kindly send your best quotation for both the website development and the relative SEO work.
Should you need any further information please don't hesitate to contact me via email or phone. I look forward to hearing from you soon.

Kind regards,
Marco Bianchi
Best Gym"

Looking at Marco's old website it's obvious that his company has potential and by working together we could really get some excellent results.
However it appears that like many others Marco has not understood that Google doesn't work like television.

"How can I come up first on Google" is by far the most common question I read when I receive a quotation request. What is very interesting is that nobody ever specifies the keyword for which they want to be first or even the reason why they want to be first.

The result of this approach is that there is a rush to spend money to deliver a message which is lacking in content and not effective.

This behaviour is explained by a cognitive bias identified by Daniel Kahneman[1] and called WYSIATI (What You See Is All That Is). It makes us consider only the variables we know of, leading us to underestimate unknown obstacles or the risk of failure.

Most people starting out on something new therefore end up being victims of the "optimistic tourist driving in the city centre" syndrome: many city centre are a confusing mass of tangled one way streets and dead ends. Taking a taxi would be far easier and safer but despite the fact they don't know the roads the optimistic tourist decides that is perfectly capable of

---

1. Kahneman Daniel, *Thinking, Fast and Slow*, Penguin, 2012.

To be at the top of Google

getting to destination. In all likelihood their nerves will get the better of them when they fails to do so and they will blame the sat-nav or even get a fine for not respecting a congestion charge area.

Lots of entrepreneurs for example underestimate the importance of effective communication and a website that can really sell their products, instead only focusing on the number of visits the website receives. It can be compared to a teenager who thinks he'll have better chances of finding a girlfriend if he asks more girls out without realising that his best bet might be to focus on what he says during fewer dates.

Everybody wants to be first on Google but most people can't even imagine the work needed to attain this objective or what it really means for Google to give a website top ranking in its results.
People are superficial in their approach.

Google aims to provide the best possible answer to a need (for information) and if we are capable of providing that by making our pages useful to users, we will be successful even without complex optimisations. Even if we are not directly dealing with Search Engine Optimization (SEO), we will see that our strategy is perfectly aligned with Google's wishes because we have the same objective: to provide the best possible answer to a specific need.

For example when you visit landing-page-effectiveness.com, you will find out that there are no other websites where an offering is developed in such a complete and easy to read manner.

This leads to Google putting my website at the top of results for a large number of keywords related to the expression "landing page". My content is simply one of the best answers to the need for information of whoever is searching. The topic is treated vertically in all its facets, the content is optimised according to a specific key and most importantly of all it is interesting fo the users.

What you must know is that Google is already perfectly aware of the quality of your website content, even before beginning to consider onpage and offpage SEO optimisation.

Google might find it sufficient to analyse user behaviour on SERPs: for example, if a user who has clicked on a link is back on the results page within 2 or 3 seconds, Google will realise that the page and its content has not satisfied the user. Google has a plethora of instruments and methods to obtain and use data. It has been doing so for twenty years, improving its results and becoming the undisputed leader in what it does: suggesting the best answers.

The objective is not to pray to God for visibility, but rather to make sure that He is the one who needs us, because it is the best for the user who is doing the search.

What results bring the user's search to an end?
What other results lead to the user carrying out further related searches?

All kinds of information is collected, analysed and evaluated. The only things to be defined are the doses of the secret recipe, the weight given to each individual factor.

If you are thinking this sounds incredible don't worry, I know the feeling. I was at the Search Marketing Connect convention in 2015 when Andrea Scarpetta and Cesarino Morellato presented the experiment through which they proved scientifically that clicks have an impact on SERP positioning and ranking.

Of course there is a huge range of factors that have an influence on your organic search positioning, so many that you would go mad trying to indulge every small change that Google implements. However don't worry, by creating excellent answers you will always be rewarded.

Improved Google positioning, just like conversions, therefore becomes a welcome consequence of a methodology and not an objective to be directly pursued in itself.

Why can't being first be the primary objective?

Focusing on the number of attempted sales rather than the quality of our offering only generates doubts about the web and the opportunity it represents. Those taking this wrong approach will eventually ask themselves questions such as:

- How can it be that with 200 users visiting my website everyday I receive no requests?
- How can it be that after spending 400 euro on AdWords I am not receiving any orders?
- If I'm not getting results, does that mean my business isn't suitable for the web?

Businesses that are unsuitable for the web do exist, but in 99.9% of cases there are two reasons why a website does not generate sales or requests:

- Users that visit the website are NOT interested in the offering;
- The website is NOT capable of motivating users to take action.

Contrarily to many publications that deal with the visibility of websites, this book will teach you to create an offering that motivates users to find out more, ask for information and make that all important purchase.

Nonetheless, profiled traffic plays a significant role and I have therefore asked one of Italy's most prominent PPC (i.e. adverstising on Google and Facebook) experts to discuss the topic in further detail and tell us more about what she has learnt about user behaviour.
However, now let's concentrate on our offering's ability to turn clicks into clients: let's concentrate on landing pages.

Why is a landing page a crucial instrument?

Getting quality traffic requires significant investment in terms of both time and money, hence making the most of the generated traffic and making sure that all our hard work doesn't go to waste, is absolutely fundamental.

A few years ago Google removed ads on the right hand side of its SERPs, bringing the number of ads, now shown exclusively at the top of the results page, down to four.

More recently it changed the colour of AdWords from yellow to green.
As costs per click continue to increase and ever less distinguishable sponsored links take precedence over organic results, managing to grab the user's attention and make the most of it is crucial.

By developing a landing page I have in some cases managed to increase sales or quotation requests even three or four fold. If we were to do just half as well with your website we would be turning it into a formidable sales system that would give us the means to purchase qualified traffic.

Imagine a shop in which there are no products on the shelves and your only option is to speak to the shop attendant. How much of a difference is a highly motivated shop attendant likely to make compared to an unmotivated shop attendant?

Most company websites nowadays are similar to unmotivated shop attendants who have momentarily closed the shop and put a "back soon" sign on the door. They won't be back at all.

Therefore, as you will have guessed, this isn't only a problem from a missed revenue perspective.
We do not only want to get new clients ourselves, we want to avoid that who doesn't come into our shop doesn't then go to one of our competitors.

A low-cost website that isn't focused on sales will not generate new contacts but worse still it will make us weaker and helpless in the face of competitors who have new revenue to reinvest.

Delegating the fate of your company is not an option. You must understand the determining factors that separate victory from failure and also increase the chances of you prevailing over the competition.

By reading this book you will find out how to make your offering invincible, putting it foremost in the minds of your potential clients so that they say YES to your conditions.

THE IMPORTANCE OF STRATEGY

> **What will we be discussing here?**
> Why must you define a strategy and not just buy instruments?
> What are the different ingredients and what is the recipe for success?

Before becoming the President of the United States, Abraham Lincoln had a number of jobs. For quite a while he was also a lumberjack.

It was therefore experience and not merely logic that brought him to say, "give me six hours to chop down a tree and I will spend the first four sharpening the ax".

Strategy and technique have a vital role in pretty much any activity.

It's the adversaries who have studied and who put past teachings into practice that we often judge to be the most talented and difficult to compete with.
This is the value of experience. It is frequently overlooked by web developers who tend to reinvent the wheel time and time again, only using their own limited personal experience.

We're so caught up in the latest trends that we fail to realise how rules and strategies that work were developed long ago. All we need to actually do is tweak and adapt them.

The importance of Strategy

At a glance everything might seem to be constantly evolving but in fact changes are only taking place on the surface. The deeper substance remains unchanged. Advertising that is successful in generating sales today uses the very same mechanisms as successful advertising from the 1960s.

There certainly is no change in decision making mechanisms that guide us in making choices and that are often related to biological or even evolutionary factors.

A very basic example of this could be aversion to risk or loss that has evolutionary origins in the sense that in antiquity it would have been better for a hunter to return home without a catch than to be eaten by a lion.

Thanks to the right strategy, attempts that have been shown to not be effective can be skipped entirely and all efforts can be focused on actions that have been proven to work. At most they will only need to be adapted: the strategy's objective is to reduce efforts to a bare minimum, to obtain greater results in less time.

You will now be learning how to choose the trees that are easiest to fell, you will be training, but most importantly you will be streamlining the key instrument you have available for building rapport with your clients: the landing page

I will be giving you a well tested and detailed recipe. The only ingredients you will have to add are the willingness to understand the needs of your potential clients and the sensitivity required to communicate with them in the best way possible.

I've called my recipe "Today the Winner is You" and it is a three-pronged approach to the sales process (also defined as a funnel) that however has only one fundamental concept at its core: the user must always be central, from the moment in which a need is first manifested in his mind to when he is a happy client ready for a second purchase after having left you a glowing reference.

My process doesn't only deal with the sales aspect. It also deals with

The importance of Strategy

what happens immediately afterwards, i.e. client satisfaction, requesting feedback and the next sale.

Satisfied clients and good feedback are a formidable boost to your confidence, to your state of mind and to the energy that will drive your future sales. They also represent the most powerful trust generating tool available to you when advertising your offering.

We are going to analyse the tiny differences that bring about huge changes. We will equip ourselves with the instruments we need to verify that all the elements of our communication are geared towards attaining one sole objective:

To optimise our users' decision making processes
so that they take action.

TODAY THE WINNER IS YOU: AIDA REVISITED

What will we be discussing here?
How is a winning offering structured? What is the famous AIDA formula? Is it still current or is it surpassed? I introduce the structure and strategy I use in my projects.

AIDA (Attention, Interest, Desire, Action) is a theoretical model developed at the beginning of the 20th century that describes how advertising works and helps implement advertising campaigns effectively.

According to AIDA the sales process is structured in four successive elements that each have a position and a specific role in helping consumers to acquire information in the correct order:

Attention ▶ Interest ▶ Desire ▶ Action

Although the 20th century gave us some fabulous copywriting techniques I choose to always use the AIDA formula as the basis for my projects, implementing it with a few extra elements we'll go on to discuss.

AIDA can easily be built upon and integrations can be made, however developing effective landing pages, without overhauling its structure or changing one its four elements, becomes extremely complex.

You must think of the decision making process as a small village shop in which all products are displayed along a single central isle and at the entrance there are just a few baskets and the cash register.

We can turn our small village shop into a supermarket (that has a car park, shopping trolleys and automatic cash registers) but will never change the proven and tested layout: the cash register will always remain at the end of the main isle, baskets will always be next to the entrance and essential products will always be a little more hidden compared to ancillary products.

The user experience offered by the shop will always be the same.
This is the secret of AIDA's success. It's just a package or a framework containing carefully selected words that have been chosen by following the cognitive process of those who will look at our offering.

Selecting these words is the copywriter's role.

To date, I think the most fitting description I've heard of a copywriter's job is what Italian podcaster Frank Merenda said during one of his Business Caffeina podcasts: "A copywriter is somebody who writes money".
It is true that unlike an author or a blogger, a copywriter works with the precise objective of selling a product or a service, encouraging a target to carry out a specific action.

Some extra elements
The problem (or need)

Thanks to Francesco Tinti I have studied copywriting in-depth and discovered that most formulas for writing effective content do not start from promoting a solution, but rather they start from the user's problem.

One of the best formulas is PAS (Problem, Agitate, Solution), developed by Dan Kennedy[2], but there are many variants all beginning with the Problem element, as it is most suitable in attracting the target user's attention.

---

2. Kennedy Dan S., *The Ultimate Sales Letter: Attract New Customers. Boost Your Sales*, Adams Media Corp, 2011.

Every day we are bombarded with hundreds of advertising messages in which all kinds of different companies offer us their solutions. This is the reason why we've stopped paying attention to communication that is packed in the form of an offering. It is only by intercepting a specific problem that we'll be able to grab a user's attention.

We'll look into this further in the next chapter, but it was important to start mentioning it because highlighting a need is already a small change to the AIDA structure that we can now call PAIDA (Problem+AIDA).

Trust

During my studies I have added further elements that improve conversion rates: building trust and removing doubt is vital in convincing the user to act and make conversion happen.

It is fundamental to get rid of any issues or doubts because as I have already mentioned we are more motivated by the fear of failure (or of making mistakes) than by potential success. Doubts and insecurities lead to inertia.

While beforehand I would use references to create desire, I now use a new formula that makes users reading my offering identify themselves with those who have already bought into it, thus eliminating any obstruction to action.

Extended satisfaction (and surprise)

Our client acquisition process ends with the action element, however in order for it to be complete, our sales funnel still requires three more elements: satisfaction, feedback and efficiency.

Extended satisfaction takes place when we go above and beyond what we had originally promised, surprising the client with something of value that is free and unexpected.

The objective of extended satisfaction is to further consolidate the established trust based relationship by proving to our client that we care. In my case the surprise could be an added A/B test, a new banner for a Facebook campaign or a landing page clone with slightly modified copy.

A user who is MORE than satisfied will spontaneously speak positively of us, whether we are present or not, maybe recommending us to friends and family to give us a bonus in trust of a kind that we'd never be able to obtain through our webpage.

Last but not least, a truly satisfied user and customer will not deny us his or her feedback.

The feedback

The users, who are now satisfied customers, have resolved their problem and have even received an unexpected surprise bonus. This is the moment in which we must ask them to share their experience with other users who find themselves in the same situation they were in before contacting us.

In the trust section of the book I will teach you the best way of using feedback, while here I will discuss the best way of collecting it, turning simple user experiences into the most persuasive references imaginable.

Funnel efficiency

At the end of the acquisition, sales and satisfaction process, efficiency comes into play.

The objective of this area of the funnel will be to reduce costs and avoid waste: not necessarily does every users come from paying sources and similarly it isn't said that the users who don't act to convert at their first visit are forever lost.

In this stage we will work on our sales strategy to understand if it is structured to maximise customer lifetime value, i.e. the total net revenue that a company can expect from a client. After all, having done so much to attract clients, convince them to make a purchase and satisfy them beyond expectations, we hardly want the relationship to end following a single sale, do we?

Today the Winner is You – A simple name to remember a method

In order to make my method's structure simple to remember I have grouped its elements according to function, creating a formula that also reminds us of our objective and way of working:

Today the Winner is You

In each stage of my process you can identify the three stages: landing, conversion and satisfaction. In more detail:

1. TODAY defines the landing stage during which the user is convinced that his search has ended because he has found the definitive solution to his problem or need. Today his problem will be resolved.
2. THE WINNER defines the conversion stage during which the user is motivated to take the action for which the webpage has been created. He must be convinced that he has nothing to loose and that he can only benefit, but he must act now.

3. YOU is needed to remind us that client satisfaction is central to our funnel, because satisfied users generate good relations that strengthen us over time and contribute to an ever more credible and competitive offering.

Problem, Solution, Interest ▶ Trust,
Desire, Action ▶ Satisfaction, Feedback, Efficiency

Landing ▶ Conversion ▶ Satisfaction

TODAY ▶ THE WINNER ▶ is YOU

You will have already understood that rather than being just a checklist of things to do, the method actually represents the ideal conversation to be developed over time with our client. There must be an adequate response for every one of our client's questions, so that he feels rewarded for trusting us and moves on to the next level of the funnel.

Compared to other systems, for example those based on email marketing, I find this method to be far more effective, especially for businesses that need to respond to a specific question (stated or implied) put to them by the market.

My method doesn't force the user to do anything and it gives the user all the time he needs. He doesn't have to give me his email address to download an e-book and doesn't have to wait for my emails to learn about the solutions I'm offering. All the information necessary for the user to resolve his problem is laid out on a single page in the most effective way possible, following a progressive process of information and persuasion.

Nowadays, any company that wants to obtain results online can't do so without email marketing, but in my method this important tool is only considered as one of the means to increase funnel efficiency that is successive to the creation of an effective sales webpage.

Why is this? Simple: as has been said previously, it makes no sense to focus on users who are not yet ready to make a purchase when we already have users who are. Nothing stops us from creating a parallel process that directs these "unready" users towards a newsletter that will give us the opportunity to nurture them over time.

Landing pages and newsletters are extraordinary instruments and debating which is best makes little sense for the time being, especially when we consider the fact that most companies have a far more urgent problem facing them: hemorraging website users.

Your webmaster told you that having a 30-40% website bounce rate is normal? Rubbish!

The bounce rate, i.e. the percentage of users that leave a website without having done anything and without having seen more than one page, is given by a website being able to effectively convey to visitors that they have found the solution to their problem.

Get ready to take plenty of notes because we will now look into how to resolve this age-old problem in the section of the book dedicated to landing: TODAY.

PART 1

The Landing Phase
TODAY

*Revealing oneself at the right time
as the perfect solution to the problem of a few
is a more effective strategy than striving to be
one of many possible solutions useful to everyone.*

INTRODUCTION

The construction of a relationship is made with small exchanges

The approach phase of a user to our webpage assumes an initial moment of uncertainty. In this moment, the users have "lent" us their confidence by clicking on our advertisement and have one main fear: to lose time (they are in a hurry) and make a mistake.

People form their own opinion on a website in the time between 17-50 milliseconds[3] and as such the first impression doesn't have anything to do with content, but the general aspect of the page, what is made clear, legible and credible.

Getting over the initial impression, we have 5 seconds to make clear to our users that we can be the solution to their problems: we must not point to an offer at this time, but only express an important possibility, that of explaining our offer.

In respect of the home page of a traditional website, a landing page has one big advantage: it must capture a single need or problem.

The second biggest advantage is that we know the problem that we have to respond to: the traffic on our landing page responds to an advertisement so that we know the expectations growing in the mind of the user.

Diminishing friction results by reducing to a minimum the gap between what the users thought they were going to find by clicking on the link and the content that they land on.

---

3. "ConversionXL" data, from "Google Research 2012".

44 The landing phase

Imagine that you catch an egg mid-flight that has fallen from the third floor of a building: your web page should make the same movement that your hand makes to intercept the needs of the users, accompanying it in the most serene way possible to the solution to their problem. You must be delicate enough that you do not break the egg, but decisive enough that you do not let it fall. Selling, in principle, is a question of sensitivity and empathy with the client.

You have probably heard talk of "cognitive fluidity"[4], an emotional state within which we are more serene and positive, trusting in our intuition and making us more obliging.
All of the blocks of information on a landing page have the same objective to stimulate this particular emotional state, reducing to zero any doubts that could take the user away from the act of conversion. To be able to carry this off, the first thing to do is to make the persons feel at ease, transmitting a feeling of familiarity with the page, even if it is the first time that they have seen it.

This perception (reliability and credibility) is also stimulated by those qualities our brand brings to the offer, but it should be confirmed when we land on the web, in the first part of the page.

The objective of the "landing" section is to exclusively manage the user's attention in the best possible way to gain their confidence and thereafter be able to present our offer.

The exchange continues between the user and the web (like a loan of attention in exchange for coherent response to a need) ending in the creation of a relationship of trust which we are going to consolidate upon during the journey to the sale.

---

4. Kahneman Daniel, Thinking, Fast and Slow, Penguin, 2012.

The landing phase | 45

Understand the phases of communication

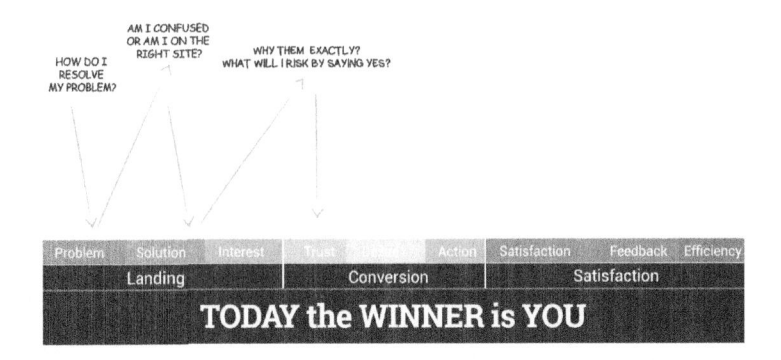

```
                AM I CONFUSED
                OR AM I ON THE
                RIGHT SITE?      WHY THEM EXACTLY?
   HOW DO I                      WHAT WILL I RISK BY SAYING YES?
   RESOLVE
   MY PROBLEM?
```

Problem	Solution	Interest	Trust		Action	Satisfaction	Feedback	Efficiency
Landing			Conversion			Satisfaction		

TODAY the WINNER is YOU

Landing, illustrated from the perspective of the method TODAY the WINNER is YOU.

If you know how to sell insurance policies you can sell cars, houses, clothes... not because you have the motivation or potential of what so many American sales coaches speak about but that in general you have learnt to listen and manoeuvre the conversation with your interlocutor.

Selling, for me, means listening. What you say doesn't have any value if you don't listen to your client. If you want to gain online contacts you can't sell them a landing page. You must sell them a system for finding online clients, and it doesn't matter if technically it's the same.

What counts is what the clients wants and what the client says.

I believe that it has been for this reason that my father has always been a great salesman, whilst I, who started at 18 years old, didn't manage any sales. In my way of selling I lacked fundamental elements.

Let's say that to create an EFFECTIVE LANDING PAGE, copywriting is not enough even if it accounts for most of the work. You have to take care of the design of the webpage, payment by clicking and the positioning of the webpage. You can't miss any elements. It has to be complete.

Enrico Madrigrano, in a fantastic course a few years ago, taught me that you should not try to sell to clients the things that they need, but also what they want, satisfying their desires.

Giulio Marsala, one of the most prestigious experts on direct response marketing in Italy added that the ideal is to "sell them what they need, dressing it up in a way so that it seems they want it". This affirmation has been repeated a lot of times in distinct books as a definition of what (or what should be) ethical persuasion: "do it in a way so that people will desire what they need".

Personally, I believe that to be able to persuade someone simply means to convince them to do something without threatening them and without the need for force, but it is not about this. It is more to do that you should offer your client something that they want, and to be able to do that, you should know the reason why they are looking for information and why they have landed on your web page.

1 – Identify the problem 49

There can be more than one reason why a user has landed on a web page, obviously, because most businesses don't offer just one single service or product.

The advantage of creating therefore, is to make the user land on a specific page which responds precisely in the best possible way to their problem.

The majority of the most effective written formulae elaborated upon for 100 years of publicity is based precisely in the pairing of "problem – solution" and for this reason it is possible to make variations or amplify these structures. Identifying the problem is always the first step of any sale.

If the user lands on the homepage of a dental studio, I can't know the reason for his visit and as a result of which I can't set out with clarity a direct message, directed uniquely at him.
If, on the contrary, that same user lands on a page for emergency dental treatment open until midnight, the reason for his visit is going to be far clearer: he is going to have pain in his molars and he is looking for a treatment that will alleviate that pain rapidly, possibly definitely, an end to his suffering. To be able to intercept the problem means that we must be sure that the first words that he reads on the website are the following (Image 1.1):

"Do you have pain in your molars? Don't suffer!
We are open 24 hours including bank holidays".

Problem, solution. Everything is consistent with the advertisement that he has clicked on.

If the service that we must promote is dental implants, the user should read something like this:

"Is smiling a problem?
"Choose the definitive solution and get rid of the pain!" (Image 1.2)

We can't land clients on a homepage, because each click doesn't direct them to a solution but would be an opportunity for them to go back in their search and resolve their problem with something else.

For this reason, landing pages are important because they are specific.

It seems like a banality, I know, but many Google Ads companies still send you to a homepage or service page which are not optimized for the contact, and above all are not constructed at their base, with the problem of the client in mind. The majority of web pages say: "I do this, and if you feel like it, get in contact with me". An EFFECTIVE LANDING PAGE, however, says: "Do you have this problem? Here you can resolve it straight away in this way".

You can use this technique with very different offers, among them: Fox Contact, for example, a software which allows you to produce personal contact forms in webpages developed with Joomla!, an open code CMS. Their principal characteristic is that they allow you to create contact forms in a simple and quick way, showing that you can be a great solution without being an expert.

For that reason, on the landing page that I have developed for the component, I haven't advertised just the function on the object, which also has very significant competitors, but the evidence that shows that this is the most simple way to create contact forms (Image 1.3).

In this way, I am not only intercepting the general problem (creating a form), **but the specific point of view from a part of the target** (which is often the most numerous and interesting in terms of sales conclusion).

1 – Identify the problem | 51

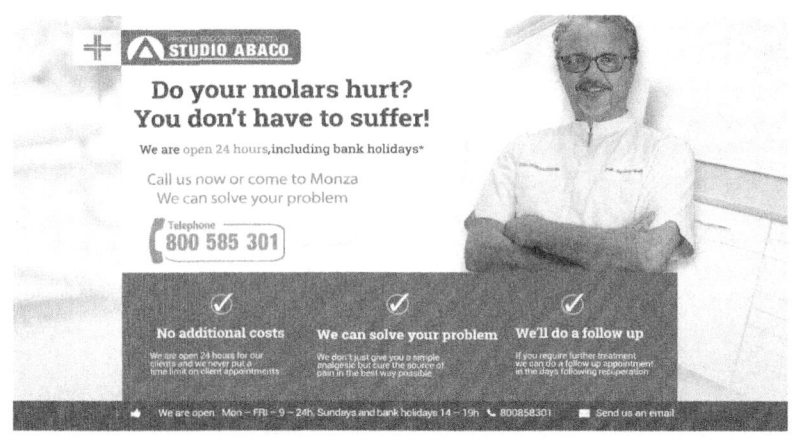

Image 1.1 - The first step should be to capture the problem of the users. The more vital and important the problem is, the clearer this needs to be.

Image 1.2 – The objective is to try and intercept the problem of the users, but we also need to capture the right blend, something which is important to the user.

The landing phase

Image 1.3 – The Landing page for FoxContact accessory

If the user don't immediately find the solution to their problem, right in front of their eyes, the first thing they will think is that they have made a mistake by clicking on the link and that they have found themselves in the wrong place and that the next result on google will be the more appropriate one.

Users have enormous confidence in their ability to find solutions and this will not work in favour of those who communicate in an unclear manner.

A small click on the "back" button and the potential client is converted into a loss. They were interested in the service and what they needed but the non-optimised web was not able to take advantage of the opportunity given to it by Google (who will certainly realise).

Understanding the problem will even allow you to improve your results in terms of offline sales, because understanding is one of the most important foundations of relationships and it is from good relationships that great sales arise.

Do you want to understand what your clients problems are?

Speak with them, question them and create specific campaigns: this is the only way to gain their attention. The capacity to easily identify a problem and reduce friction to a minimum during the landing phase is one of the main reasons why a landing page is so effective, and a home page, by contrast, so complicated to design. The problem is the heart and the balance point on which the whole page is built and defines the orientation of all elements, such as the truth or controversy that we will talk about later.

But first we should face another obstacle. Not all of our clients are the same and they do not share the same problem.

If, in effect, molar pain can affect us all in the same way (making us all behave a little like scared children), the majority of products or services don't cut it and it is probable that your clients from one to the next will be very different. Different people correspond to different needs and different ways of understanding the same problem.

To identify a concrete requirement better, we should group people together in types with defined profiles.

Define the service target

Profiles and archetypes are a useful tool which enable us to "put ourselves in the shoes" of our potential clients to try to adjust our offer to each person. In reality, this process should be started BEFORE we develop whichever product or service, but I know through experience that this does not work like this. The majority of people who create products or services believe that they only have to worry about this issue marginally, only later to come up against market rules:

*One of the things that I hear said to business
the most is that their product or service is suitable
for any of the public, but this, for me, is a problem.*

Whatever your product or service may be, it will never be the appropriate solution for everyone, and there will always be people whose purchase is more appropriate than others. These potential clients can be grouped together and represented by a profile "model", character or archetype.

Think about this book. If you are an entrepreneur or an internet operator you can gain great knowledge and understand how to direct your communication to results, knowing which activities take priority over others.

But what if you were an expert in web marketing or landing pages? Probably for you the advantages of reading this book would be less and your opinion about my work could be less positive, although of course you could appreciate, for example, the structure, the method or the examples that accompany the explanations (or I hope so!!).

Similarly, if I go into too much detail, I could run the risk of making my work inaccessible to less advanced users.

The objective of this book, therefore is to simplify sufficiently complex and evolved concepts so that any entrepreneur can understand them and follow them step by step, a path that will lead to the creation of a landing page. For me, the biggest difficulty is to define the level of detail for a non-technical person so that they will find it "tolerable".

I have used precisely this example because a number of years ago, I made a mistake by judging a book too banal, until I later understood the book was not appropriate and adapted for me. It is like when we are younger and we say "how disgusting!" whilst our mothers argue with us saying: "no, it is not disgusting. We say: I don't like it".

The author had done an extraordinary job of spreading the word, making all these complicated concepts accessible and opening doors to the web to lots of people. That's why sometimes we don't understand the reasons for commercial successes, whether they are films, books or services: it's a problem of targeting, and precisely for this reason we need to lend out attention to this aspect.
In order to understand the problem of who is going to visit your landing page and create the best response possible, you should, above all, know

your potential clients. You could therefore, find yourself in either of these two situations:

A. Your business has been working for a long time and you have a good idea of who your clients are.
B. You are starting your business from scratch and you don't have feedback upon which to base yourself.

In the first case, my advice is to create profiles based on the clients that have been the most satisfied with your service or product.

Let's say that you have a little bar on the beach and for food you serve meat or vegetarian hamburgers. All your clients who try the meat burgers are left unsatisfied and they complain because they don't taste of anything, whilst the ones that try the veggie burgers are ecstatic and they leave excellent online reviews. At this point, it seems obvious to me that you have two possibilities:

- Improve the quality of your beef burgers
- Take the beef burgers off the menu.

Without going into the merits of brand positioning, which we will take a look at later on, we are going to try and imagine the clients of your small business and by defining the profiles know which is the best way to act.

Here you have some examples:

- Max is 55 years old and works 5 minutes on foot from your business. He is single and likes to stay slim and has a lot of energy. Mostly after eating and when at work he is subject to a lapse in attention. He normally eats out three times a week and during his lunch hour he uses a tablet to catch up with work and answer emails. He's been vegan for a long time and he prefers eating where they don't cook meat.
- Clara is 33 years old and has stayed at home since she became a mother. She lives near to your business and she is sporty, although, ultimately

her baby takes up a lot of her time. Precisely for this reason, she takes advantage of lunchtime to see her friends and ex-work colleagues and spend a bit of time chatting with them. She doesn't have a particular preference about food but she doesn't like restaurants where they take your food away whilst you are still eating your last mouthful, not least because she likes to eat in peace.
- Philip is 27 years old and works in a call centre in the same building where your restaurant is located. He spends all morning on the telephone and come lunchtime his head is ready to explode. All he wants to do is lie down on the soft grass and close his eyes for 20 minutes to relax. He frequently meditates and is interested in alternative culture. He looks after his diet and although he is not vegetarian, he avoids meat wherever possible.

Now we have defined the three types of client, we should look at identifying which kind is present in the field within which you operate and furthermore, construct an offer in accordance with their needs. Focussing on the three types, we can guess that Philip and Max are compatible with each other and a quiet restaurant where they can eat in peace will make them happy, especially if they cook good healthy food that doesn't include meat.

Philip, furthermore, works in the same building where the restaurant is situated and alongside him there will definitely be other men that will share a similar profile to his. The only thing that might not fit in with our plan might be Clara, who next to her friends and baby, could make the atmosphere a little bit noisy. A good strategy could therefore be to construct the communication based on the points in common between Max and Philip. In this case, the problem or need that sticks out would be:

How to be able to eat a light healthy meal that doesn't include meat in a relaxed and quiet setting. As a concrete example of this type of work, may I quote the work developed by Meetab, that produced personalised food supplements.
By means of a certain specific test you can find out exactly your nutritional characteristics in order to construct a precisely personalised supplement plan.
You know that those adverts that explain nutrition to you have to be perso-

nalised but even still they divide the world population into four categories (generally, women-men, young-old)?

Meetab produces supplements that are truly tailored to your nutritional needs by answering these questions: "Who are you? What type of supplements do you need? And the most important, what is it that you wish for?"

For Meetab, we identified three client profiles, that we can summarise as follows:

1. Student, 20-25 years old that wants to improve their sports performance;
2. Manager, 40-42 years old that wants to be more productive and shine at work;
3. Woman, 30-35 years old that wants to lose weight and improve her self-esteem and relationship with her own body.

In this case, the same product has three very different types of client. How can you develop an effective offer for all of them?

The answer is very simple: you can't.

You should consider vertical communication for each target, creating a message that is directed uniquely at each one of them and using images that they can identify with (see images 1.4, 1.5 and 1.6).

Image 1.4 – The landing page made for Meetab which targets the student athlete who wants to improve their results.

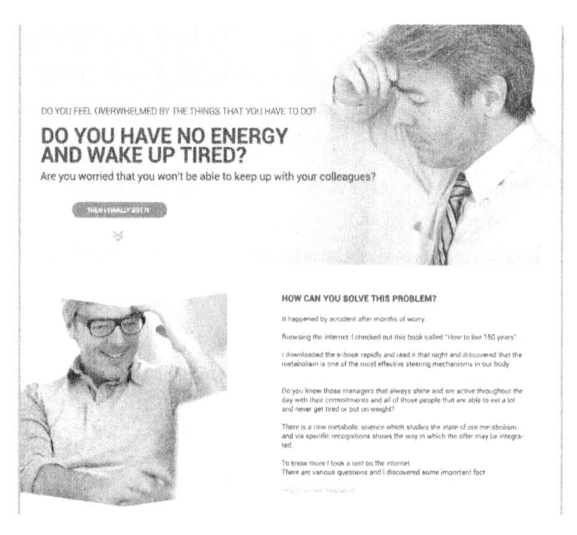

Image 1.5 – The landing page made for Meetab which targets the manager who wants to improve their productivity

1 – Identify the problem | 59

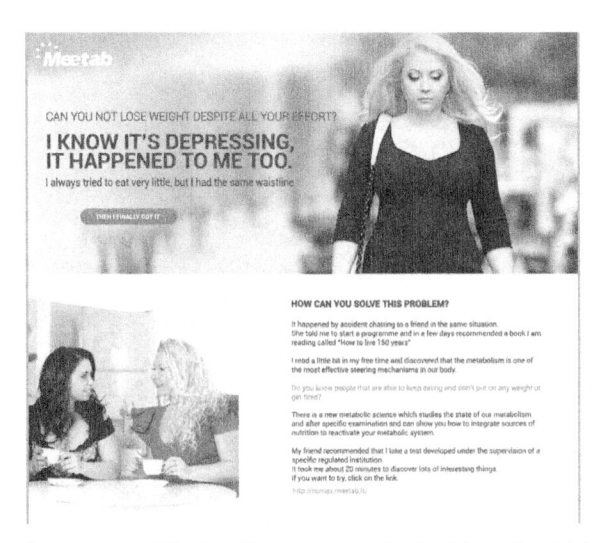

Image 1.6 – The landing page made for Meetab which targets the woman who wants to improve their relationship with their body.

ADVICE FROM THE AUTHOR

At this point at the end of each chapter I recommend that you take a break.
If you have 15-20 minutes I suggest you go to the support page (https://landing-page-effectiveness.com/gym/) to put into practice the concepts set out and to better assimilate the information I have given you so far.
All you will need is a simple sheet of paper, a black marker, a highlighter and a pen.
With these exercises you can start to design your page, which you can develop as you read the book. Of course, it is not going to be the final one but it will be a great help to start translating these ideas into a design.

See you soon! https://landing-page-effectiveness.com/gym/

CHAPTER 2
THE RULES OF ATTRACTION

What are we talking about here?
How to manage the user's landing to reduce the amount of friction, guiding the user's attention in the best way between the text and the images.

One of the most delicate areas of the landing page is the first part of the page where the user sees that he is landing on the web and clicks on the advert. This is defined as "above the fold" and gets its name from the slang for printed press, where the first part of the page of a newspaper would be where you would find the most important parts of the paper. Imagine you have a newspaper folded vertically in two, the fold would divide the first page into the top and bottom sections of the newspaper.

On a web page, this fold constitutes the screen tip and is considered "above the fold" all of those aspects that the user can see without the need to scroll. In comparison with the printed press, we can obviously suppose that our task presented some additional difficulties.
Not every screen is the same!

The landing phase

A well-developed web page should be capable of automatically adapting to the devices which display it and in the launching phase special attention is paid to the three main modes in which it will be displayed: desktop, tablet and smartphone. In each phase, we should bear in mind that on average the most popular screens are between 800 – 1000 pixels. Generally I dedicate between 500-600 pixels to the top part and between 200-300 pixels for the bottom part.

In each zone, as we have seen before in the previous images, we are going to publish various elements:

- The business logo;
- a representative image;
- the problem, the solution and a description of the solution;
- the "call to action";
- a band with three elements (general advantages);
- a navigation menu which leads to the anchors on the page;
- Symbols linked to the action area .

The images

Knowing how to choose the right image for the part "above the fold" of our web page is fundamental. It's not just about having a professional image, but about conveying the right feeling to our users.

The image in the above the fold section, like everything we do, should have an objective: it has to make our user feel like they are in the right place.

The first rule to follow should always be that of coherency /friction. If users arrive on our web page via campaigns that use images (for example, those of Facebook, or from the Google Display network), these images should be identical or as close as possible to those that we will find above the fold of our landing page.

Also, in this case, in the same way as copy, we can use PPC campaigns to verify which image is more effective (we create the same insertion, modify only the images, present them to the same target and observe which one gets more clicks).

In my experience, an image should have at least one of these functions (in order of importance):
A. a. show the object of the offer, possible in use;
B. b. excite the user, transmitting the benefit received;
C. c. represent the professional or expert who will provide the service.

A. Image that reflects the benefit of the product

Of all the telesales that I have seen in my life, one of the most effective, without doubt, is the one of chef Tony and his knives Miracle Blade. In the advert, that maybe you might remember, you can see the chef manhandling the utensils and moving with ease between the various distinct plates until he opens an aluminium can. By showing the product whilst you are using it permits the person who sees the advert or the website to project themselves into the future and think about the benefit of the object or the service that would support their life.

If we manage to make the client imagine what their life would be like thanks to us, we can tie them to our offer by taking advantage of the feeling of loss that would mean to leave the page.

The best strategy is to have the product used by the person whose profile corresponds to the offer target. If, for example we are selling a pushchair that is especially designed for partners that have twins and we want to attract the mothers, on our landing page we should publish a photo of a 35-year-old mother smiling whilst pushing the pushchair with two children.

On Facebook we can make an advert which appears to all the mothers aged between 35 and 40 years of age.
If, on the contrary, our target is the grandparents who look after the grandchildren (perhaps they want to give a gift to their children), our objective would be all women between the ages of approximately 50 and

64 | The landing phase

65 years of age and the image we choose should be of an older couple peacefully walking.

Identifying the target is very important, and for this reason it is fundamental to know your own clients and who makes the decisions at the time of buying.

As we have said, we should be as specific as possible, but this does not mean giving up on a part of the target; we can for example duplicate our landing page and we can recreate it in a distinct way for each of our possible objectives.

The most important thing which is key to our communication, is the object or service that we want to sell, or even better, the benefit that our user will receive from our offer.
(Image 2.1).

Image 2.1 – Yango's potential clients want to achieve a younger and healthier appearance and be in good shape without having to resort to cosmetic surgery. I have therefore set out in the image an attractive couple who are in shape upon which the target can project their own future.

Victor Schwab, in his book "How to write a good advertisement"[5], describes how this strategy focuses on how the demonstration of the use of the objects increases the probability of capturing the target's attention as well as their willingness to purchase.

B. The importance of emotion

Another element that we should pay our attention to is the emotiveness of the image that we publish. Wherever possible our image should always transmit an emotion. A lot of people argue that emotion is the only springboard that can push us towards action and that the only function that our rationality has is to make us believe and to justify that this is the best option.

Perhaps we are not all completely and totally emotional, but this aspect remains of paramount importance and we shouldn't underestimate it. If it is easy to be sure about what is transmitted by a text, an image lends itself to subjective evaluations and we should be sure that it is coherent and in line with our message, enriching it with all of the things (emotions, sentiments, dreams) which are difficult for the text to transmit.

Say, for example, we rent an amazing villa, ideal for holidays with friends, if we publish photos of the villa with people enjoying themselves, it is more likely that people visiting the page will request information.

When I worked on the landing page for a surf school in Fuerteventura called Onemorewave, I looked for various images that would be able to effectively transmit a fun day with Stefano and Alessandro.

Perhaps the photo of a guy or a girl on the same precarious stage of take-off on their first wave would have been more appropriate (when they get to their feet and start surfing) in order to capture the emotion, but in the end I preferred a group photo where you could see the guys smiling and enthusiastic after a day spent together
(Image 2.2).

---

5. Schwab Victor O., *How to write a good advertisement*, Echo Point Books & Media, 2013.

66 The landing phase

Image 2.2 – Surfing is difficult. The principal objective of a day with One-MoreWave school is to have fun together. For this reason I have chosen a group photo (Http://onemorewave.es/it/)

Image 2.3 – In a project for Nika Island Resort, I highlighted a different aspect: the advantage of being able to enjoy your own private beach and the privacy that it offers (http://www.offerte-maldive.it/)

Publishing a photo of one of the teachers riding a big wave in Bali would of course have been more impressive, but how many people would have been able to identify with that? We should not choose the nicest picture but the one that will be more effective in communicating the advantages to our users, an image that they can identify with.

To favour the objective of being able to get numerous interested group bookings rather than just a single contact, I decided to place sporting performance (and the difficulty of being able to surf) in the background of doing something fun with a group of friends.

With the project for the Nika resort in the Maldives, I chose a distinct path, highlighting the real differential elements of this island in comparison with the rest: it is the only one where you can count on a small private beach (Image 2.3).

C. Representing the professional who will provide the service

In the example of the landing page developed for a surf school, I mentioned the fact that the main image that we publish can contribute to the type of enquiries that we receive, but is this really the case? I discovered through my own endeavours that it is possible to influence the type of enquiries more than you could ever imagine.

This is what happened many years ago when I started overlaying the Futura Immagine brand to the professional, Luca Orlandini. I took about 300-400 photos from which I was able to take a decent one and put it on my home page, wearing a nice blue t-shirt depicting a very 'Silicon Valley' style. "Most of the people that contact me – I thought – will already know me somehow or will have read my articles, I'm not young anymore and it should work"
(Image 2.4).

68 The landing phase

Image 2.4 – Home page accompanied by a photo of me in a blue t-shirt

It worked. I received the same number of enquiries, plus some more so I gave the makeover the thumb up and approved it.

Something strange happened… My "type of client" had changed: if before more structured businesses had contacted me, now with my new image it seemed to work more for independent professionals and young entrepreneurs.

"Wait a minute", I thought, "Are we saying that the t-shirt influences the type of inquiries? "No, this can't be possible…"

So, I did a test, I changed the photo of me in the t-shirt for one more respectable, with a suit and tie. Well, more or less. I live in Fuerteventura and I have left all my suits in Italy, so I resorted to Photoshop for some touch-ups (Image 2.5).

It could be just a coincidence (in which case, I would count on statistics to see whether there is a scientific explanation), but using the photo with the suit and tie, I started to work for more structured businesses. Straight after, I substituted the artificially modified photo for a real one, something a little

2 – The rules of attraction | 69

Image 2.5 – Home page accompanied by my touched-up photo in a suit.

Image 2.6 – Home page accompanied by my photo in a "real" suit.

less formal and more natural (Image 2.6).
The interesting thing is that the photo doesn't influence the number of inquiries itself, but only the type of client that contacts me and accepts my quote. One small detail is enough to radically change what your users think of your offer: think about it when you choose the main picture of your landing page.

When is it best to put our picture?

For the user who lands on the landing page, the best solution is always to be in front of the product or service, but this is **NOT ALWAYS** possible.

In my case, for example, it would be impossible to find an image that my target audience could identify with (because each page is designed for a specific target).

Publishing the photo of the professional can be a valid solution for several reasons:

- creating trust saying: "look who I am, I am putting a face to my service";
- transmitting authority;
- allows us to re-establish the link with those who already know us;
- it saves us from having to use a banal stock photo free of publishing rights.

The image should explain and emphasise the text

I often see landing pages where the image takes up all of the headline and the text, and as a result, text is written on top of the photo.

Aesthetically, the effect is nice, but in practice the text is not very legible and makes the user tired, without adding anything relevant in 8 seconds out of 10. The situation is even worse with the presence of a video, but the problem comes from a poor approach to web design. The design does not aim to "fill the page" or "impress the user", nor does it aim to offer an original navigation experience, the objective of the visual in the section above the fold of the page is ONLY to favour the reading of our header and the click on the button that invites the user to action (or call to action, abbreviated as CTA).

> *On a landing page the main focus are headline and the CTA, not the photos. The aim of the images must be to create a context and reinforce the concepts expressed in the headline.*

The title, subtitle and benefits must always be clearly visible, well separated from all the other elements and clearly distinguishable.

2 – The rules of attraction 71

To make you understand the importance of images in the section above the fold, I will analyse three good resources that will allow you to create landing pages without technical knowledge: Unbounce, LeadPages and Instapage.

While the first two resources look very similar (Images 2.7 and 2.8), Instapage has opted for a different solution (Image 2.9).

Looking at the section above the fold in Image 2.7 it is hard to understand the product: what are they offering me? The text presupposes that I know what a landing page is. Will it be like that for all the web users or will someone go backwards, without understanding what is being talked about? I have two call to actions to choose from, with different actions, which one do I choose? The text in negative (white on blue), does not make easy reading.

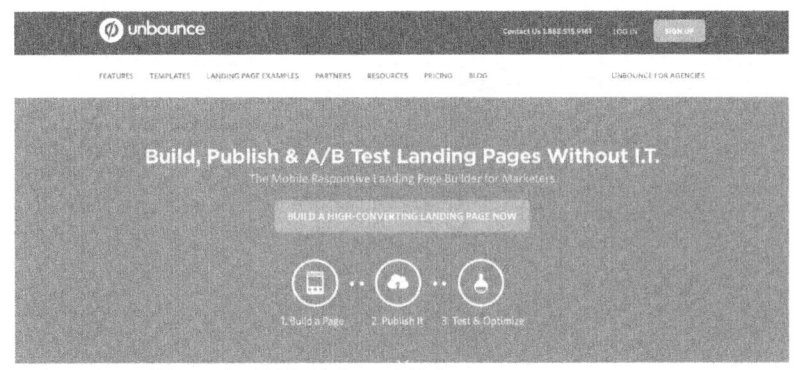

Image 2.7 - Above the fold section of Unbounce.

Studying the section above the fold in image 2.8, we see that it does not mention the product, but only the objective. Do you deal with landing pages, e-mail marketing, or statistics on user behaviour? Compared to the previous website, it is even less clear. I have two calls to action, but here they are less coherent. The background image is totally useless and only makes reading more difficult.

72 | The landing phase

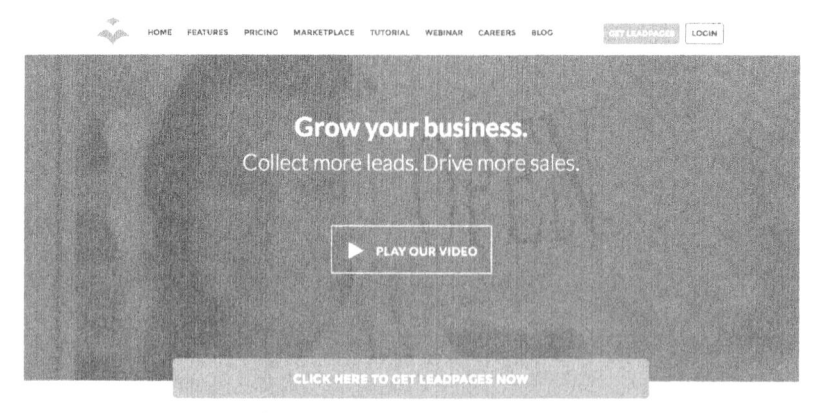

Image 2.8 - Above the fold section of Leadpages

Ok, they make me design a webpage: in the above the fold section of Instapage in image 2.9 finally it is clear. At first I can see the results which I can obtain and also see one of the advantages (the pages are responsive). I have a line of text which highlights one of the advantages (the ability to create the page quickly and one single call to action which compels me to begin immediately. Note that the text on the left can be read much more easily than the central text and that an Instapage image which can help the interested potential client to understand the service.

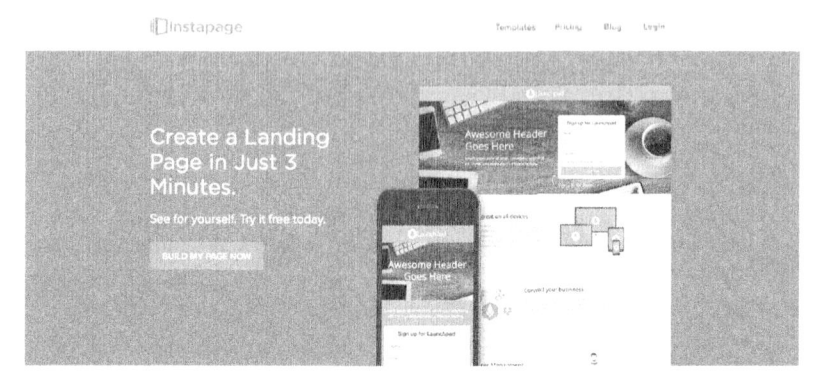

Image 2.9 - Above the fold section of Instapage.

If the photo is of a person it should look at the CTA

The human brain is inevitably attracted by human faces. According to some scientists, all of the area of the brain called fusiform gyrus is dedicated to recognising human faces.

Thanks to our natural and innate ability to recognise human faces, we can amuse ourselves by playing games like seeing faces and expressions in the clouds, in the stains on a tablecloth or objects. Who hasn't done this at some point?

A human face on an advert or on a web page is always going to capture our attention at first glance, gaining priority over any other text or element on the page.

This means that on a page full of adverts, the one that has an image of a face will be viewed before any of the others; but also, if we put only a line of text and a photo on our page this could detract from what we are trying to say. If the person in the photo looks directly at us our attention will be captured even more because, instinctively, when anyone looks directly at us, we feel the need to understand why, subconsciously deciding whether they may represent a threat. We can't help it.

Just think that in some social experiments, a simple poster with two eyes looking out, can completely change the behaviour of the person looking at it. Feeling observed, the participants in an experiment were more likely to leave the table in a fast food restaurant as tidy as they found it behaving themselves like they should... and none of them realised that it was due to a simple poster that influenced their behaviour.

On our landing page and in all communications which should attract attention, we should always have in mind these characteristics of the brain, taking advantage of, and using this in our favour to the maximum.

Avoiding direct looks and choosing subjects that look or point towards elements with which we want to draw our readers' attention, can guide the user's attention in a natural way towards the elements that we consider more

74 | The landing phase

important. By substituting the image and comparing the two headings, the difference is immediately obvious, confirming all that has been shown in eye-tracking tests.

Images 2.10 and 2.11 – in these images we can see the attention difference that the human eye lends to the two images (the stained parts indicate the areas where we spend more time looking at). If in the first version the most observed area is the child's face, in the second version, our attention is drawn to the text that the child is looking at.

2 – The rules of attraction 75

In the last version of my landing page, for example, I turned my eyes towards the text precisely to guide the user's gaze (Image 2.12).

Image 2.12 – On my landing page, as well as turning the gaze towards the title, I have selected the photo colours to match the logo and above all, the call to action stands out (https://landing-page-effectiveness.com)

How to check that the image is suitable

To check that the image expresses the concept well, you can use the Usabilityhub five second test which you will find at the address fivesecondtest.com. This test allows you to show a screenshot to 5 people at random for 5 seconds and afterwards ask them questions like; "What would this page sell?" It's a very easy test to use, above all, when you have used a photo of the product or service in the image or have indeed demonstrated the benefit people can obtain from it by purchasing your offer (naturally it is less effective if you just put up a photo of the professional).

If you want, as an additional step, you can translate the above the fold texts (including rapid services, like One Hour Translation) and try the test again.

It is fundamental that the page target can understand the theme being dealt within 5 seconds. If the results of the test are inconclusive you should continue working on the page.

> Note
>
> The type of person to whom the page is shown is also relevant when it comes to the purpose of the test. With Usabilityhub, finding people completely within your target will be more difficult but there is nothing to stop you performing a 5 second test in the real world. The sample will be smaller but will certainly be more in line with your target.

Above the fold copywriting

Everything that we have done up until now is intended to make the text evident in the upper half of our landing page, one of the most important parts of the whole page. It contains the user's problem, our solution and above all, the principal reason that they should use us and our unique selling proposition.

At this moment, we still haven't captured our user's attention, and like a cowboy in the wild west would do with his gun, they are ready to click and return back, clicking on one of our competitors.

To quit now would be a double loss: in addition to losing a user, Google takes these actions into account in its quality assessment; if a lot of the users behave in the same way, we are not going to be a good resource for them. In addition, our quality level in Google Ads or our organic position in Google searches can be adversely affected.

But how important actually is the copy? Truly, a lot.
Your writing skills determine 80% of the effectiveness of the landing page.

Claude C. Hopkins[6], one of the first "scientific" advertisers argued that the value of an agency comes from its experience and from the cases it has already tackled which allow it to know what works and what doesn't.[6] Naturally, we are talking about direct marketing and communication aimed exclusively at selling and not at advertising the brand.

For more than 100 years of advertising, numerous tests and experiments have been carried out; even before Google Ads and its A/B tests were invented in ads, discount coupons and mailing lists were already being used. Through the analysis of the results of a lot of campaigns, it has been possible to define the procedures and best practices which work and those which differ from all those communications destined to "make show" or simply to "make the name of the company known". Knowing the history and having developed a case study allows us to identify which paths are safer than others and which techniques have given more "scientific" results for those who have used them. Experience has a very important role in communication and being documented in historical cases is GOLD for those who carry out this work.

If we think about the importance of experience in determining the success or failure of a communication tool, we will have a lot to think and smile about from all those web agencies that let the client choose the design of the website. Those who do not draw from studies or experience in communication cannot know what works and what does not work, and rely solely on their own personal taste.

This "discharge of responsibility" cannot work for those who set out to create the Invincible Offer.

---

6. Hopkins Claude C., *Scientific Advertising*, Midwest Journal Press, 2014.

Confidence has to be absolute and it is important that the results and the strategic decisions inherent to the project are in the hands of those with the specific experience and not those in charge of the job.

A few years ago, for example, I worked with a dental client that wanted to use at all costs a design thought out for a photography studio but in their case the huge photos couldn't work and when they realised that I was right I had to sort it out and come up with a solution.

> *It is very important not to get carried away by taste and emotions, and to always structure our work according to what we have learned from studies and experience without underestimating anything.*

Think about how many elements we have seen so far in only the first part of the page. Could you have imagined that you would have to pay so much attention?

The writing of the texts is even more complex: whilst for an image or a colour scheme the client can rely on their own aesthetic taste, copywriting requires sensitivity and a deep empathy with the people who are going to read our text.

Because, as we have already said, the salesmen are the words.

I'm going to tell you about an episode taken from The Small Big[7], the last book written by Robert Cialdini, so you can see clearer how an effective text can make a decisive contribution to the effectiveness and outcome of communicative action.

His consulting agency, the Influence at Work team, was contacted by the tax administrative body in Great Britain, Her Majesty's Revenue & Customs (HMRC), to try to reduce the number of citizens who were late paying their taxes. HMRC had already put in place various policies, focusing on interest on arrears, sanctions and legal action, to try to reduce the number of citizens lagging behind, but with little success.

---

7. Martin Steve J., Goldstein Noah J., Cialdini Robert B., *The Small Big*, Profile Books, 2015.

"Influence at Work" managed to reduce the percentage of clients lagging behind from 57% the previous year to an incredible 86%. If the previous year's percentage had remained unchanged, without the intervention of Influence at Work they would have collected almost £190 million less in revenue.

Do you know how they managed to get this extraordinary result?

By adding a simple sentence to the standard letter to those trailing behind with payments each year. The beginning of it was: **"most recipients have already paid their taxes"**. Little by little they perfected the result until arriving at a last version to which was added the name of the city where the recipient lived: **"the majority of Brighton citizens have already paid their taxes"**.

If you think about it, it's just a sentence, but with this example we can see how copywriting can motivate a person to do what you ask of them. In this case, Robert Cialdini revealed how you can take advantage of the principle of social proof to bring a person's behaviour into line with others[8].

A bit later on we are going to see how we can take advantage of other means of persuasion codified by Cialdini to motivate the user into immediate action increasing the conversion rate of our site. But first we have to define the above the fold text adding the second most important element after "the problem": our unique selling proposition.

The unique selling proposition

The unique selling proposition[9] is the holy grail of effective communication. It was developed at the beginning of the 1940's and allowed its inventor, Rosser Reeves "to increase invoicing from 40 million dollars per year to 150 million dollars without his advertising agency losing a single customer and achieving an exceptional level of sales.

The USP (unique selling proposition), which can also be defined as "an element of uniqueness that motivates the purchase", which consists in fact

---

8. Cialdini Robert B., Influence: The Psychology of Persuasion, Harper Business, 2006.
9. Reeves Rosser, Reality in Advertising, N W Widener, United States 2015.

of an EXCLUSIVE (and desirable) advantage which our competitors do not offer or do not communicate.

The unique selling proposition is divided into three parts:

1. Each advertising campaign should propose a benefit to the consumer and not only through words or assumptions or embellishments. Each advert should say "buy this product and you will get this concrete benefit".
2. It should be a benefit that the competition can't offer or doesn't offer (although this works even if the competition offers it but doesn't let you know about it). It should be unique, exclusive whether it is a product exclusivity or a proposal that is not used for advertising in that market sector.
3. The benefit should be so strong to push millions of consumers to buy it and in the process attract new consumers towards the product.

USP collides with one of the principal market problems, undifferentiation between products, which leads companies to struggle with the only variable over which they have risky but quick control: the price.

Creating an Invincible Offer therefore begins with a huge job of understanding the product or service to be sold and its consumers.

If in the first phase we were able to identify the problem, now we have to extract the EXCLUSIVE reason that our solution is better than all the others: I speak of "extraction" because often, the characteristic of uniqueness is already present at the base of what the company offers and only needs to be highlighted.

2 – The rules of attraction

I remember an interesting presentation by Francesco Tinti in one of the most important webmarketing convention in Italy, in 2014, in which he spoke about copywriting and an analysis of the webpage of the Michelangelo de Milan hotel from which he extracted a unique and strong sales proposition but one that was never communicated: this hotel in Milan has a conference room measuring more than 1.300m2 and is only 30 seconds from the Milan central station.

The interesting thing that Francesco highlighted is that very often at the end our client takes this characteristic for granted and doesn't include it in its communications. But they know it. In that presentation, which I wholly recommend that you take a look at, there are many interesting examples of USP, like for example, Johnson's shampoo, which doesn't "sting your eyes", or that of the "waterproof" Timberlands or indeed Club Med "the first all-inclusive holiday".

USP really works when it manages to position a company in first place in the mind of the consumer because of its element of uniqueness. Others may copy it, but they will not be the first. The uniqueness can refer to the concrete offer but also the brand. When a brand offers products or services oriented towards its own positioning in the market, maximum results are obtained in terms of efficiency.

FuturaImmagine has been dealing with websites for years with a high conversion rate, and all the services it provides are sales-oriented: landing page, usability analysis and persuasive copywriting. This feature allows me to convince those users who get to the bottom of my landing page and click on the link that leads to FuturaImmagine to investigate the company behind the offer further. When they see that the company's business is totally focussed on selling (and not on generic things like website development or e-commerce creation), the content already transmitted from the landing page acquires even more value.

Returning to our unique selling proposition, what is not going to work as an element of uniqueness? Surprisingly, what is working the least, are especially what is suggested the most: quality, to be the market leader, low prices and customer service. The majority of these characteristics don't provide uniqueness, something which could be difficult to perceive, or even something that customers take for granted.

One of Reeves' most famous adverts using the USP technique is the M&M's, which "melt in your mouth, not in your hand," which is still used today.

"No Sir, I'm not saying that charming, witty and warm copy won't sell. I'm just saying I've seen thousands of charming, witty campaigns that didn't sell.".
Rosser Reeves

How to write the headline

After identifying the problem and defining the unique selling proposition you are left with just the headline missing which you find exactly between these two elements (in the order of reading: problem, title, unique selling proposition).

In my EFFECTIVE LANDING PAGE, the headline should achieve two objectives, often in contrast to each other

- It should attract the user's attention (being written in the biggest font);
- It must contain words used in the positioning of Google or in the scoring of Google Ads

Up until now we haven't spoken about it, but once the page is published, I'll have to deal with the systems that bring traffic to my offer. If we exclude the page name in the browser, which is probably the most important on-page element, the following section is above the fold and we don't have much text!

To create a clean and easy to read text we are forced to write only a few words so this will be effective for the user. Personally, I wouldn't advise you to write a headline ONLY for Google… but I think it is important to bear in mind that what we write is going to influence our visibility and the

2 – The rules of attraction

way in which users do their searches won't always correspond to what works best for copywriting.

In order to find an equilibrium between users and search engines, I often use the headline to enunciate the main word and make it visible in the place where I want to position myself, which, in general, corresponds to the name of the solution I offer.

We'll soon see how we can prove which combination works best, but first we'll take advantage of the advice of one of the most famous publicists of all time, John Caples[10].

A pioneer in the application of the scientific method in advertising, he used the split test in the early 1940's. Caples, like many hard-sell pioneers, used discount coupons sent by mail. By analysing the returns in terms of the use of the coupon, he could understand which copy was more effective 60 years before Google Ads made its appearance in the advertising market.

John Caples argued that he could spend hours or days on a single headline, but as soon as he found it, he knew his work was almost done.

> *On the average, five times as many people read the headline as read the body copy. When you have written your headline, you have spent 80 cents out of your dollar.*
> David Ogilvy

---

10. Caples John e Hahn Fred E., *Tested Advertising Methods*, Prentice Hall, 1998.

The headline is what makes the user decide to keep reading or abandon the page and for this reason it is very important. A good headline, as set out by Caples, is more important than a nice photo and it is not essential that it is synthetic but it is however essential that it transmits everything that we want to say.

If you have used clickbaiting technique (a headline writing technique that pushes users to click and visit the website), you will probably know this advert that Caples made a long time ago before the internet was even imagined (Image 2.13).

Image 2.13 – "They laughed when I sat at the piano but when I started to play..." One of the most well-known direct marketing headlines of all time was written by John Caples in his first year as a copywriter.

John Caples identified 35 formulas for writing headlines that work; some of which involve the use of words that capture attention, for example:

- "new", "now", "finally";
- "what to do for", "how", "why";
- "yes", "advice", "this", "which".

In an effective headline the following also works:

- Adding a date;
- Using a news style (like a newspaper);
- Mention a special price, easy payment, special offer;
- Tell a story;
- Offer useful and valuable information;
- Offer a free trial of the product or service;
- Warn the user that it is better to wait to buy or invest;
- Do it in such a way that the manufacturer speaks directly to the client;
- Ask the reader a question (I use this technique to enunciate a problem);
- Offer advantages by way of verified facts or believable images.

In his sacred book of copy, Caples also indicates some things that we should avoid if we want to obtain results, like poetic writing, the element of surprise or finally anything which lacks credibility.

If you want to achieve results when you write, you should write in a simple and direct way:

To impress your offer on the mind of the reader or listener, it is necessary to put it into brief, simple language... No farfetched or obscure statement will stop them. You have got to hit them where they live in the heart or in the head. You have got to catch their eyes or ears with something simple, something direct, something they want.
John Caples

Testing and improving the above the fold copy

To check whether we have properly defined the texts of our offer we can use Google Ads to do an A/B test: by configuring the rotation of the adverts in a homogeneous way, we can easily test different copies to see which one works best. The main advantage of using
the A/B tests on Google Ads compared to that on the landing page is that with Google Ads we only pay for the click, but we carry out the tests considering the idea as a whole.

Let me explain it better. Let us imagine a case where the user costs me 1$ and I decide to use 1000 users to carry out a test knowing that version A will obtain double the clicks of version B (660 clicks versus 340 clicks).

Using the Google Ads system, I will pay for the clicks received (660 $), whilst doing tests on the page, the user must land on the web anyway and as a consequence, the cost would be in equal to the value of the total sample (1000 $).

Having lower costs allows me to use larger samples, obtain more data and therefore implement more efficient tests.

To consider a test valid I have two options:

- If the difference is enormous (for example 700-800 clicks in A and 200-300 clicks in B) I will consider the test valid when I reach a sample of 300 clicks on a single option;
- If the test reveals little difference (less than 15%), I try to let it run for a longer period of time or I consider it valid when the sample becomes really important.

We should always consider that coincidence intervention, like our small samples, could lead to misleading results. For those that want more depth, there are formulas that allow us to calculate the statistical confidence of a test (a percentage number that tells us how much a test is reliable).

How to proceed with the copy test?

1. The first thing I do is test the problem. I create three variants in which I write the same problem in three slightly different ways, in the headline of the advert. In the second and third lines I write the same headline and the same promise, so the only difference is in the title.
2. Once the problem is defined, I keep the same headline and continue the test with the promise in the last line of my Google ad. I try to extract four main benefits from the service or product and then I test four adverts.
3. The advantage that comes out as the winner is inserted into my promise, while I add the other three in order of importance as callout extensions.

These tests RULE over my copy. The page should be perfectly coordinated with the advert, and once the tests are finalised, I will apply my "discoverings" to the above the fold copy.

Optimising attention

We have already defined the copy and the image that will accompany the header of our website, what is left to manage in the best possible way our user's landing on our offer?

Optimising attention.

Each element placed in our above the fold has an "attention cost" and it is very important to be sensitive enough not to overdo it and eliminate every possible distraction, so as not to overload the attention of whoever lands on the page. Now it is time to highlight the most important concepts, reduce the visibility of any accessories and be sure that all elements contribute to a single purpose: make the user assimilate our message and motivate him to go into greater depth.

The landing phase

When we speak about advertising, the assimilation of the message is fundamental, but it is equally important WHAT PART of the message is assimilated.
Hundreds of messages reside in our memory that we are not even aware of but when we see a gorilla emotionally playing the drum solo of Phil Collins'track 'In the Air tonight' the connection with the famous Cadbury's TV commercial is immediate.
But…..what did that advertise promote? What product?
What were we supposed to do?

If you don't remember it, it is probably because these catchy sketches have eclipsed the product or brand (the Airtel phone company).

The visual shouldn't replace the copy

A photo that is too colourful or that is too detailed can have the same counterproductive effect. The principal objective should be to emphasise the concepts expressed, enriching the headline and helping the user to imagine the words that we are describing.

The colours should be homogenous and there should not be disturbing elements because they steal attention from that which is most important: the call to action. From the webpages screen shots published in this book, you will note that even though they are in the grey scale, how the elements are always in equilibrium: I have taken great care to ensure that there are not too many elements to make your tired, reducing to a minimum the cognitive load necessary to assimilate information.

The photo colour schemes, lightly saturated will constitute the palette base of the page. Since the base colour on which we will place the writing is white (it is the simplest and easiest solution to implement), we can use darker colours for the text or titles and lighter ones for additional boxes or shadows. To extract the colours you can use a normal sample or free online services like Pictaculous, where, introducing a photo you will obtain a colour scheme.

On the page photo, http://dentifissi.studioresta.it, the base colour used is water green with hexadecimal code #3dc2b8 (to visualise the colour you can visit the page https://landing-page-effectiveness.com/gym/).

With this colour, I did the background of the square with the three main advantages and the logo, while I used a slightly darker colour with the same tone for the fixed bar of the contact section. Also, the background upon which you have the blank supposed page on which the offer is based has the same colour tone but much lighter.

Image a photo in grey scale, like the ones published in this book with just one colour. Can you imagine how the resulting page would look? This element would be like a button calling our attention.

Utilising a scale of homogenous colours you would be able to obtain exactly this effect even using images that are not black and white.

Your page will have a more professional look and playing with the contrast you will be able to make the disparity between the images more or less evident (Images 2.14 and 2.15).

If it is true that the visual should never replace the copy, it is also true that it should start from the bottom of the page, otherwise it is useless and dispensable (for this reason I never use images or, even worse, videos for the background).

If the elements of the page are well differentiated, it will be easier for the reader to define the reading areas, and therefore, to quickly visualize the content, capturing at a glance the subject treated in the page.

We should always remember that we only have a few seconds: the user's opinion is created in one twentieth of a second and if he doesn't feel like he is in the right place between 4-5 seconds, he will leave the page.

90 | The landing phase

Images 2.14 and 2.15 – Two versions compared: the first shows the actual colour scheme and the free telephone number and the second by contrast optimises the base colours to click the CTA (http://dentifissi.studioresta.it).

2 – The rules of attraction 91

In image 2.16 you can see a screen shot of the actual online home page of Instapage and in image 2.17 you can see on the other hand how some quick corrections that I have carried out can make the communication of the site more effective (I advise you to visualise these photos on the full page: https://landing-page-effectiveness.com/gym/).

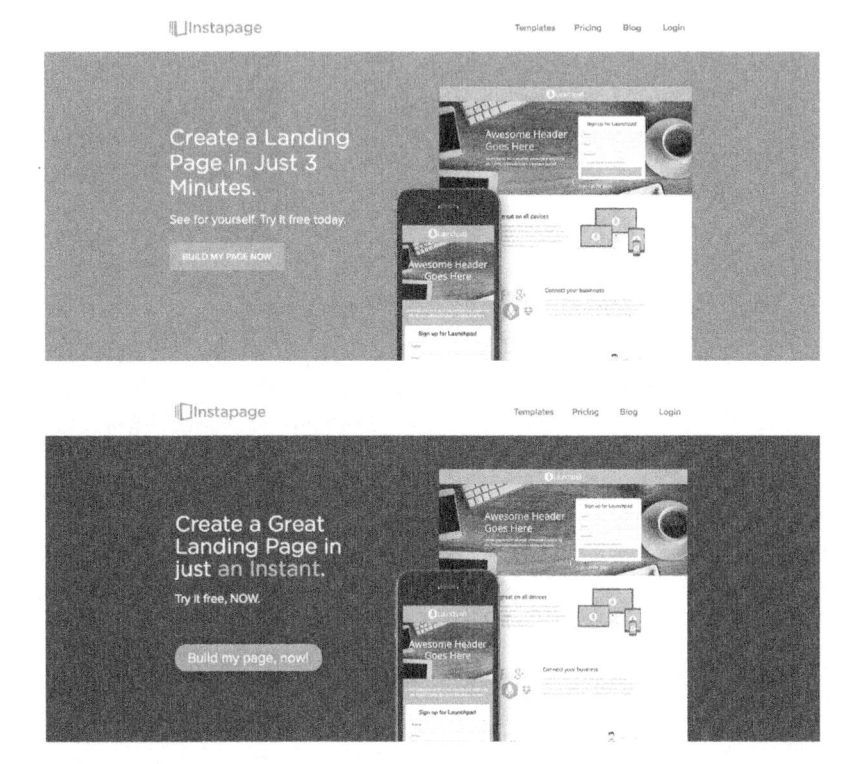

Images 2.16 and 2.17 – two comparative versions: in the first, the original, the background colour is very similar to the logo and that used in the image. It doesn't allow the text to stand out and makes the page seem quite flat. In the second, which I have optimised, you can read the text better and the image has more impact, but above all, the call to action stands out from the rest of the page and is easier to find.

Highlighting the call to action (CTA)

On the Studio Resta page I didn't have a call to action button (the objective was to receive telephone calls from the free number) but if I had added a CTA button what colour would have suited the best?

The most simple and direct solution is to use a complementary colour. By using a tool such as Adobe Colour, the hexadecimal code can be easily recovered.

In this case we are going to see that the complementary colour is reddish orange, colour #3dc2b8 (you can see the colour scheme at the address http://adobe.ly/1mcykhc).

To highlight the CTA in the header, making sure I am not mistaken, I could use an orange rounded button with white letters.

The rounded contours in the buttons fulfill the objective of keeping the user's eyes inside the lines (the angular edges can be perceived as indicators or arrows) and the colour would make this element stand out from the others in the header... but there could be a problem.

If on the one hand it is important that the CTA is in a stand-out colour, it is equally important that this colour doesn't work to block. While it is very visible, I rarely use a fire red colour for CTA because it is a warning colour that conveys a "be careful" message and interferes with cognitive flow.

To optimise the contrast, you therefore need to be careful and choose a photo whose complementary colour don't rely on one of these shades: I don't want my user to suddenly come out of his "cognitive fluency" state alarmed by a colour that requires attention!

The best solution, since each of us has our own aesthetic taste, is to find a colour that stands out, and then do A/B tests with the content of the page to decide whether we have done a good job or if we need to make it more legible.

In the above the fold area, the user should be able to easily see the following information in order of importance:

1. **His problem,** translated into an attention-grabbing question or statement;
2. **The headline,** or indeed the "salvation" and thus the solution to their problem (principal keyword);
3. **The promise (or USP)** and then offering a guarantee, where possible with an element of uniqueness;
4. **The introduction** to the call to action (if it's necessary)
5. **Call to action** principal.

How do you transfer this information to an effective above the fold section? The following is an example used in the project "toll-free-number":

> **Problem:** do you want a toll-free-number?
> **Headline keyword:** numeroverde800[11]
> **Promise /USP:** try it for 10 days and keep it if it works
> **Introduction CTA:** it works. 108,000 businesses have increased their contacts
> **CTA**: set it up and try your number!

The page is already full of text so I moved the advantages a little further down the page, creating a dark green band where I set them out in several places (images 2.18 and 2.19).

The optimal solution would be to put the bullet points further up in the white part with the text, but I preferred to take advantage of the main area for social proof (the sentence about the 108,000 companies that have already activated a green number).

It is an ongoing war to ensure that the user does not get tired and is able to take in just the right amount of information. It is important to just say enough without overloading the page with too many elements.

---

[11]. "numeroverde800", the Italian version of our toll-free number service

The landing phase

On the MACfaaast it was easier. The users' problem in this case was the slowness of their Macbook or iMac and thanks to the services of Giancarlo it is possible to return them quickly "to life".

Image 2.18 – On this page you can see how the weight of the typeface helps to identify the most important elements and how the CTA is always highlighted, even with a lot of text (www.numeroverde800.com)

Image 2.19 – divide the advantages into three macro zones and by making a list of all the important points makes it much easier (and probable) that it is read by the user (www.numeroverde800.com).

The scheme of the information is simpler:

1. Problem: Slow Mac drive you crazy?
2. Headline /keyword: We can speed it up
3. Promise /USP: New life for your MAC with SSD and OSX optimisation

2 – The rules of attraction

4. Advantages: We can even speed up an old MAC – 100% satisfaction guarantee or refund – paid the same day
5. CTA: How quick can it become? (leads to the sample video)

The most important thing in this case as well is to reduce the amount of information provided to give more importance and visibility to the remaining information (image 2.20).

Image 2.20 - Above the fold section on the landing page of 'Macfaast' website

Each additional element takes away from the most important element; Rosser Reeves himself warned the copywriter about bringing the secondary advantages too close to the unique selling proposition to prevent the latter from losing momentum.

The promise and the call to action should always be the strongest points of the message.

Look at how attention is distributed on my landing page and how it changes if we try and take away some of the less important elements
(Images 2.21 and 2.22).

96 | The landing phase

Image 2.21 – Above the fold with all the visible elements (www.landing-page-effectiveness.com)

Image 2.22 – Above the fold with elements reduced to a minimum (www.landing-page-effectiveness.com)

Can you see how it is made easier for the reader in the second screen shot? And they think we're talking about an optimized header I've been working on for months! You obviously cannot sacrifice everything but we should always get rid of those elements that are irritating.

It is true that the landing pages should not have a browsing menu?

I am in agreement with the general opinion that en effective landing page should not have outgoing links, but at the same time, I notice that the majority of users are disorientated if they don't find a browsing menu.

What can we do? I often publish a simple menu with just a few descriptive elements which allows the user to feel comfortable, like a softly caressing hand that whispers "don't worry, everything is going to be alright. Fill in the contact form."

The ideal is to understand how much value a browsing menu adds to your page. Does it help to understand what you are doing? Does it help users to browse? Do they use it? Is it good that a user jumps straight to the offer without reading the further content? For example, I am almost convinced that the terms OFFER or PRICE on the menu, at least in my case, do not apply, because my clients' acquisition motivation is not about a competitive price, but the expected result.

This is precisely the point upon which I reason to decide whether to publish a menu or not: do I really want my users to jump all the process that leads them to understand how I have established my prices?

The terms "price" and "offer", are by far the most clicked on in all the landing pages I have done, and so therefore we have two options:

A. We make sure that the exclusive features of our offer are repeated in the price section, so that even those who jump directly to the price have a complete overview at a glance;

B. We avoid publishing the menu to force the user to go through all lanes that make up our minimarket.

There is even in this instance no absolute answer about what is the best way to proceed because it changes with every product. The best we can do is an A/B test with Optimizely to compare the results of identical pages that differ only by the use or non-use of the browsing menu.

What page do people spend more time on? Which page generates more conversions?

How to test the above the fold section

As well as the 5 second test there is also a 5 step test. Placing yourself 2-3 metres from the screen, you should be able to identify the most important elements on the page and understand what it is about and what you should do (the invitation to action). It's not only about writing some things in large type, using a strong contrast but about writing in smaller type creating well-defined "zones" that are easy to distinguish: the menu zone, the teaser zone with problem – solution – promise, the invitation to action and the advantage zone.

I usually use a very large bold font (Slab or Serif) for the headline (h1 and h2), and a large sans serif font for the question and promise (h3). On the web texts are usually 16 px in size which I use except when I want to write about something in more depth which can often go unnoticed by the reader because it has not been considered important.

If looking at my landing pages from a distance you don't get a sense of confusion but you can understand what the page sells and what you have to do, the above the fold design works and we can move on to the next step.

On the in-depth website you will find an article full of updated examples of font combination.

Did you know that each font communicates differently and by using one or the other could even influence the credibility of your offer?

2 – The rules of attraction

ADVICE FROM THE AUTHOR

At this point at the end of each chapter I recommend that you take a break.

If you have 15-20 minutes I suggest you go to the support page (https://landing-page-effectiveness.com/gym/) to put into practice the concepts set out and to better assimilate the information I have given you so far. All you will need is a simple sheet of paper, a black marker, a highlighter and a pen.

With these exercises you can start to design your page, which you can develop as you read the book. Of course, it is not going to be the final one but it will be a great help to start translating these ideas into a design.

See you soon! https://landing-page-effectiveness.com/gym/

CHAPTER 3
THE RULES OF INTEREST

> **What are we talking about here?**
> How to create a trusting relationship with the person who reads our offer by making good use of video, incontrovertible truths and progressive information.

Fortunately, the phase dedicated to interest is a little simpler and less critical. We have gained the interest of our user, he has clicked on our CTA or he has scrolled with the mouse to know more: we can take a deep breathe and launch our attack.

In this area we should describe our solution clearly and directly, using understandable terms and mentioning one by one the benefits which the user can expect to obtain.

Many people, when they write, tend to talk about technical features but if we do this the reader will be less emotionally involved. I don't want to say that you can't be specific but, for example if you think about an insurance policy, writing "covered up to 5 million $" is far less effective than "you will be safe from anything that happens" or better still "you will be safe from anything that happens (up to 5 million $)".

It's the security that sells, not the amount.
The amount is just an intensifier.

Avoiding el WYSIATI

The aim of this section is to show that what you offer is much more complex and articulate than you might think at first interest. Like we said in the initial section dedicated to strategy the human brain is influenced by a cognitive distortion called WYSIATI, an anacronym for **What You See Is All There Is**.

In actual fact, we as human beings have a tendency to minimise the difficulties of any task which we are unfamiliar with, overstimating our ability to succeed. Kahneman elevates this prejudice to an "engine of capitalism[12]". If a person opening a new business realised just how few his chances to succeed were in the face of the difficulties that he had to overcome he would probably give up in an instant.

In the case of our offer, this bias is a problem. If we sell a valuable product or a quality service, we will probably take into account all the elements necessary to satisfy the customer and we will therefore always have to fight against those who offer a similar product at a lower quality but at a lower price. We run the risk of losing all the customers who prefer to "spend little".

If the majority of your clients don't understand the difference between what you offer and what your competitors offer the issue faced will probably be how you can motivate them to buy from you.

Try to think about your opinion about landing pages and the web pages before reading this book. We are only in the first third of our journey and halfway through the development of the landing page but you can see already how many traps there are. Your estimation of the investment needed to develop an effective project has probably already changed, and you're starting to see that an incredible landing page cannot be achieved with an investment of between 3000-4000 dollars to be able to transmit contents to a sale offer.
The objective of the area dedicated to interest is then to describe your product or service and the reasons why the user should choose you, in

---

12. Kahneman Daniel, *Thinking, Fast and Slow*, Penguin, 2012.

the most complete and synthetic way possible. In order to keep our user glued to the screen we have three weapons:

1. Presentation video;
2. incontrovertible facts;
3. progressive information .

Unlike the first two elements, which can be presented indistinctly in first or second place, the last element is always progressive information: a specific order in the explanation of my offers allows me to achieve a great level of consensus.

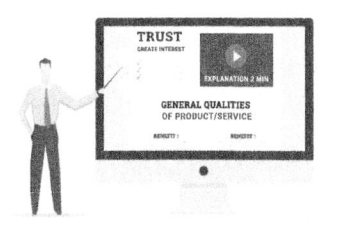

At the end of the interest area, maybe the user still doesn't want to buy but it is now clear to him that our offer is precisely what he was looking for. But let's start with one of the most appreciated things in my landing pages, so much so that I have created a special service all on its own: the presentation video.

The presentation video

One of the most effective elements is the presentation video. Since I started specialising in landing pages I have done a lot and managed to give optimal results in terms of the effectiveness of the page. Videos are amongst the most used elements in landing pages in any country. They work as a vehicle for the delivery of quality content. It is not the video that works, as it is not the landing page: it is the way the tool is used.

Some sellers post the video directly below the headline next to the contact form but I prefer to place it further below in amongst the first elements of the interest area.

A good heading with a good image already allows me to satisfy the initial question: "Am I in the right place?" The fact that they are scrolling will allow me to get more points on my confidence care scoreboard.

The rules to follow are simple. An effective video should:

1. Explain the service in a maximum of two minutes, starting with the problem, highlighting your unique selling proposition and talking about the benefits your customers are looking for and consider important (not the benefits to you though, so watch out!);
2. speak to a single, specific user and not to everyone at the same time. Use a direct language, as if you were talking to a friend (exactly as in the landing page), except for some particular and concrete cases;
3. it should have rhythm, be fresh, rapid and professional. It should be cheerful, it shouldn't be boring and definitely not "theoretical". It is important that it is well done: it is not enough to mount a PowerPoint presentation in mp4 to have an effective video;
4. you should do it after the landing after having collected some data with the A/B tests and having verified that our copy works. The video is an extension of the landing and increases the efficiency of it, but if the copy and landing are not well done it won't be useful at all.

A lot of people think that a video cost is prohibitive but it's not like this. With approximately 800-900 $ you can create a great video in two minutes that you can even use to promote yourself on YouTube. The effectiveness of promoting yourself on this platform varies depending on the sector, the offer and the quality of our video, but the costs are still bearable (unlike the search network) and worth trying.

The problem with videos is finding someone to translate into animation the concepts which are expressed by the copy.

This is a difficult job which requires creativity, especially when the person in charge of the editing does not speak the same language as the message is written in. I tried out professional sites and companies before

I found James, who has the advantage of:

- Being able to translate my ideas into scenes, using clip art in the best way possible (in short, editing and creative use of clip art, if the video has a limited budget);
- Being very careful with the synchronisation of the voice with the scenes. If I do a list of the advantages with bullet points he is good at showing these advantages in sync with my voice.
- Being very careful with the spelling and the accents. It can seem obvious but it's very annoying to have to send an edit back three times with error modifications and each time waiting, for example, 10 days for the video to be sent again ;
- Using different styles and in the end putting together a video with music in the background which makes it professional and gives it rhythm.

The last important point to have in mind when filming the video is the quality of the audio. In my first video I used a low-quality microphone and although an audio expert made the sound better, the result wasn't very good. Now I use an Apogee microphone which records the voice with much cleaner sound.

In my offer I have included two videos, both done by James with a "blackboard effect": the first video is posted just after the above the fold, whilst the second is at the end of the page, after the contact section (with the form and telephone number).

If the objective of the first video is to explain the offer in a simple and quick way, the objective of the one in the final part of the page is to eliminate the user's last doubts that remain after the contact form.

We'll talk about the closing video at the end of the chapter dedicated to "desire after action".

106 | The landing phase

Image 3.1 – Frame of the video which explains my service and presents it in less than two minutes (www.landing-page-effectiveness.com)

Incontrovertible truths

The incontrovertible truths, as long as they can be used, are very useful, because they fulfill the function of "shaking up" the target's problem, already expressed in the first part of the page and before the advertisement.

The formula "problem – agitation – solution" was elaborated by Dan Kennedy in his bestselling book "The Ultimate Sales Letter" and is one of the most effective copywriting structures of all time. According to this formula, after having understood the target's problem, you must first amplify the disturbance to then provide the solution.

3 – The rules of attraction 107

In the disturbance part, you can in this order:

1. aggravate the state of the matter and the urgency of finding an immediate solution;
2. make a list of the consequences that could arise as a result, acting as a verification for what might happen if the problem isn't resolved immediately;
3. disqualify solutions offered by the competition to the point where they don't offer a solution.

Only at this point can you show your solution, alleviating the pressure generated on the user. These are a few examples of incontrovertible truths:

- If we sell a natural system to increase the defences of the immune system, we can talk about how the pace of western life weakens us through routines in which stress makes us sick (and the time lost to illness causes us even more stress);
- If we sell an anti-theft system, we can provide data that tells us how much thefts have increased in the target area and how traditional anti-theft systems are now ineffective (unlike GPS, whose effectiveness is taken into account even in insurance policies);
- If we sell a system to make an iMac quicker, we can explain how it becomes inexorably slower each time we update with OSX (and how other remedies can make things even slower).

All of this information can obviously be supported by a video extracted from the news in links to reputable sources or in verifiable data. They are called incontrovertible facts because the user should not have to think about whether it is true or false but considers all of what is said as a fact itself **which aggravates their problem.**

The landing phase

A little while ago I developed a landing page for a service that sped up Macs by way of the substitution of the hard drive for an SSD. I also had this problem and was therefore quite informed on the subject. Once again, it's not about ripping off my clients: the substitution with an SSD is the only really effective solution to speed up a Mac. For this reason, just at the start of the interest phase, I published three incontrovertible facts:

- **TRUTH 1**
  The majority of programs to speed up the Mac only damage them and apart from not being able to make it quicker can also make its features worse (link to the official Apple help page).
- **TRUTH 2**
  With older models most of the slowdown is almost never caused by RAM which is generally sufficient and is used only by some applications.
- **TRUTH 3**
  If you really want to increase speed you should substitute your HDD for an SSD..

Following on from these three facts (the first one even has an external link that points to the support section of Apple's website), I put in a video in which I PROVE the fact that a laptop is much faster after changing the disk).

16 seconds to start, compared to 39 seconds filmed before the change.

The video was so effective, that once the landing had been delivered my client produced dozens of them, one for each model of notebook, to show to whoever contact him the video for his specific machine.

In this case, the truths are published BEFORE the video, because the video is the proof of the third declaration. In the case of a different service, they could be published at the side of the video, or even after: you have to assess each individual case. The best thing is to do tests and think about what goes on in the mind of the person who will see the page

(asking for opinions from friends and acquaintances who do not know the subject generally leads to good ideas).
It's important that this two elements are always at the beginning of the Interest Area.

Progressive information

After having "agitated" the problem with incontrovertible truths, now we should describe the possible solutions, providing the users with all the information they are looking for.

I repeat: all the information that they are looking for.

Won't this be too much? No.
I still remember an amazing Marketing course when they said that all the information on the page is never too much and you have to deal with all of the aspects of the theme, even those which seem obvious and banal: "if users are overinformed they can always buy but those that do not find the information that they are looking for will never buy".

A lot of people ask me if it is better for a landing page to be long or short, a page graphically austere or care in each detail and I simply respond without hesitation: **a long landing page is better.** Even if a short landing page can get results (and cost less in terms of effort), the same offer has also been proven to be most effective on a long page.

It has been discussed at length by the best advertisers in the world during the golden years of advertising that **a long WELL WRITTEN text is more effective than a short one.**

> *Direct response advertisers know that short copy doesn't sell.*
> *In split run test, long copy invariably outsells short copy.*
> David Ogilvy

Information is important. We can't dispense with it if we want to make an EFFECTIVE LANDING PAGE, but precisely because we should write more, we must give the information in the correct order. I like to call this section "progressive information" because first I always describe the general advantages of the solution (also common to my client's competitors) and at the same time the specific reasons why they should choose me.

If, for example, I wanted to sell a page that sells the development of web pages using WordPress, I could structure the content progressively:

1. **The general advantages of CMS:** CMS open source allows you to have a professional web page saving a lot of the costs of development; the average cost of a project developed with CMS is one quarter of that of a tailor-made project (data)
2. **The general advantages of WordPress:** it is easy to install, equipped with automatic updates, has professional themes at low prices and it's easy to get help on.
3. **The specific advantages of my offer:** I have many years of specific experience, I will make your website more secure against attacks, easier to navigate and visually more attractive (data or references to confirm what I say).

In point 2, as you can see, I describe the advantages of WordPress, not of my service, as if I were to say: "to be 100% clear you could obtain these benefits even if you develop your web with someone else, I'm just saying that you've done a good job by looking up information about WordPress". My user has probably already heard about this information and read about it on other websites.

Starting from the most generic truths and continuing with more and more concrete advantages, I will give confirmations of the facts, adding

SPEAKING OUT AGAINST YOUR OWN INTERESTS

If we are also capable of offering alternatives, for example, the development in Joomla, we can include a sentence that "speaks out against our own interests" to encourage telephone contact saying something like:

"If you want a multilingual website or believe that your website could grow in terms of funding, the best option for you would be to use Joomla! not WordPress. Contact us now so you don't make a mistake and make sure you choose the tool that best suits your needs, WordPress is fantastic, but there is no better CMS than Joomla!

In this case we have the possibility of getting a direct phone call from our client and soon be able to send them our best offer. A distinct element that differentiates ourselves from all the competitors that can't offer both CMS. Speaking against our interests and in particular against the product we are promoting allows us to appear more credible and reliable when promoting its advantages.

Personally, if I had to give my advice I would ALWAYS choose Joomla! (it's more stable, more expandable and has a better managed add-on market), but it would be difficult to explain this to a customer looking specifically for WordPress. Similarly, I could create a box on the Joomla! page in which I advise users to contact me if they have never used a CMS before and prefer a simpler solution like WordPress.

The first time that I heard talk of this technique (speaking out against your own interests) it was in the Filippo Toso's short videos. I had always found this technique very interesting and powerful but obviously we should also be capable of offering a credible alternative making it desirable.

The landing phase

Returning to our progressive information I would like to show you what I did for Donatella, an independent distributor for Herbalife in Rome. In the first place I explain why it is important to complement your own nutrition and afterwards I speak about the advantages of Herbalife and only at the end the concrete advantages of Donatella (Image 3.2).

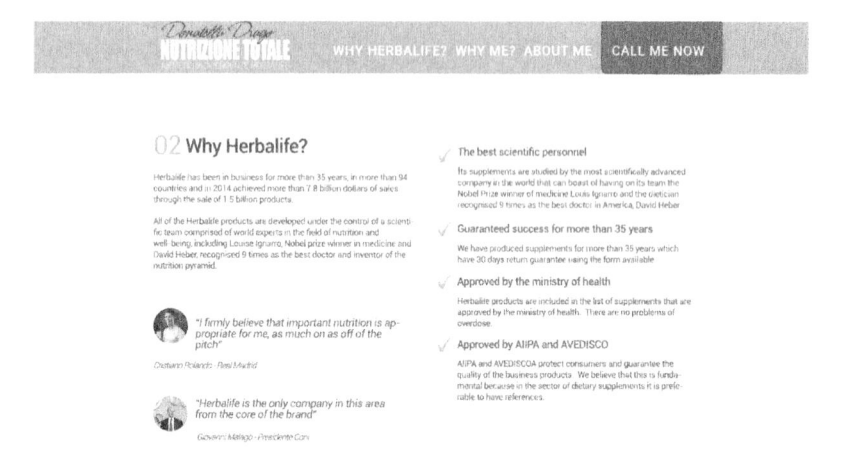

Image 3.2 – typeface for an independent Herbalife distributor: on the left I have written a few explanatory paragraphs and I published two important testimonies about the brand (the process in this case was: why you should complement nutrition, why Herbalife and finally why one should direct towards my client); on the right I have provided a point by point summary of the principal advantages.

In case it is not possible to use the progressive information technique, it is possible to use a different strategy. Already highlighted above the fold on the landing page are three principal macro advantages in increasing level of importance inside the section dedicated to interest. In the project "Wood Constructions" developed for Greenbuild for example, I introduced the three principal advantages at the beginning of the web page, briefly summarising after I'd gone into further depth once the user had scrolled down (Images 3.3 and 3.4).

How do you make the video text more legible?

The area dedicated to interest develops after the fold and is generally characterised by the need to publish a lot of information. For this reason, it is essential to create a nice page design, introducing all the information that our user needs before performing the conversion action. The appearance of the page and the care you have taken will also influence the result because it makes an offer more credible and reliable. What am I referring to when I say that even with the same content, a "nice" page can become an "ugly" page?

And furthermore, what do we understand by a "nice page" and an "ugly page"?

When we speak about the look of a landing page I am not only referring to the simple aesthetic appearance, but also to the level of detail and the coherency between the elements that make up the landing page which augment the results, for example:

1. Legibility of the text which can reduce user's fatigue;
2. the selection of typeface fonts which can help to distinguish important information from that which only acts as an accessory;
3. the space between paragraphs, which should be short and well separated;
4. the images should be professional with descriptions supporting and interlacing with the text.

114 | The landing phase

Images 3.3 and 3.4 – the above fold sections of the effective landing page for Greenbuild. Just below the header in the highlighted section I have listed the three advantages which are also in the browser menu. The informative structure of the page follows the order, extending the concepts summarised in the initial paragraph and treating all the possible facets of the topic.

3 – The rules of attraction

If a programmer gives more attention to the technical aspects of programming then a web designer tends to care more about the design. Often the people who could get the best results (those who are good at writing copy) lose contacts with web pages that seem to have been made by my grandmother with Word. These offers, apart from belonging to a small sector (in general, training), are not very effective because they are immediately pigeonholed in our brain in the same place where we place the advertising leaflets that we find in the mailbox when we get home at night.

I'm not saying that a landing page of this type can't work but using it today would be like going out on a Saturday night with a Oldsmobile Cutlass. The Oldsmobile Cutlass was really nice in the 1980's but now our tastes are a little more refined and the people that look at our web pages are accustomed to seeing something with higher standards.

Being a marketer does not mean having to make "commercial" offers and having the possibility of saving something does not mean that it is compulsory to carry out projects in 10 minutes (although lately showing off the little time it takes to write messages that make you rich is very fashionable). Waiting to have a perfect page to approach the market is a mistake, but it is an even more serious mistake to publish something of little value. You need the right balance. Let's look at some basic rules.

- The text should be divided into paragraphs with a maximum of 3-4 lines. You should avoid publishing more than 3-4 consecutive paragraphs without interspersing them with a title that gives an idea of the content of the paragraph.
- Each paragraph should have a maximum of between 500 and 600 px (it shouldn't occupy the whole line).
- The text font should be san serif (like Ariel or Helvetica to make us understood) with a minimum size of 16 px if we use a 400 frame and 18-20 px if we use a 100 frame.
- The line spacing should be 1.3 - 1.4 larger if the paragraph widens or the font size increases.

The landing phase

On the Personified website you will find an excellent article in English that constitutes one of the best guides on the legibility of web typeface. The ideal in the desktop view is to divide the information on the page into two or three columns which will end up being two as it appears on a tablet and one on a mobile, following the rules of responsive design. Graphically, I recommend that you use a list of fundamental points which are clearly visible with green tick symbols or numbered lists. In this phase the user is likely to jump from one point to another on the page and key points are an effective way to present the content. This generally works well with lists that contain 3 to 5 points and not more for each information block. I recommend that you always take care with the typeface and don't create sentences with more than 3 lines and distance them well between each other.

As I have already said, it is essential to always talk in terms of the benefits and only later on about any technical characteristics of a product. For example, if we are talking about a monitor:

- "Resolution WQXGA 2560x1600 (4096k), the most available in the market",

is less effective than:

- "Incredible experience thanks to be the best resolution possible (2560x1600,4k)".

The first rule of web pages creatin that motivates users to read it is to avoid text walls and dividing the content into a lot of small individual portions. If on the one hand it is possible to write long texts, even 15-20 lines, on the other hand we must give our users clear visual signals that allow them to understand the content of the text, in order to let them decide whether to skip it or not at first glance. Sometimes it is necessary to write a lot but this is not an excuse to overload our user's attention with unecessary informations.

The rejuvenation program offered by Yango for example, is difficult to summarise in a few words. Unlike major dietary supplement programs that are more or less the same for everyone, Yango is based on metabolomic studies, a new science that analyses metabolism in a specific way. To be able to create the correct "dose" of information we should act on two fronts:

- On the one hand, we should offer the user who wants to go more in depth with all the information that we consider necessary in legible text and well divided paragraphs;
- On the other hand, we should offer more pressured readers the chance "to jump to conclusions" thanks to our descriptive titles and list of key points that summarise all the advantages of the program (Image 3.5).

If you notice, the titles and key points have a bigger and more prominent body. The text on the left is important, but a hurried Internet user might need to choose, and the typographical hierarchies allow me to make this task easier.

In case additional information is required, the only and last solution could be to use a modal window that could be opened as an emergent window like a pop-up which the user clicks on "to get more information". This technique allows us to keep the page tidy, but also to know what is most important for the website users (we can know how many have opened this window), as well as to modify the page to give priority to the information that is most important for the reader. The more we know the users, and the more we give them the information that they need, the better chance we have of doing it well.

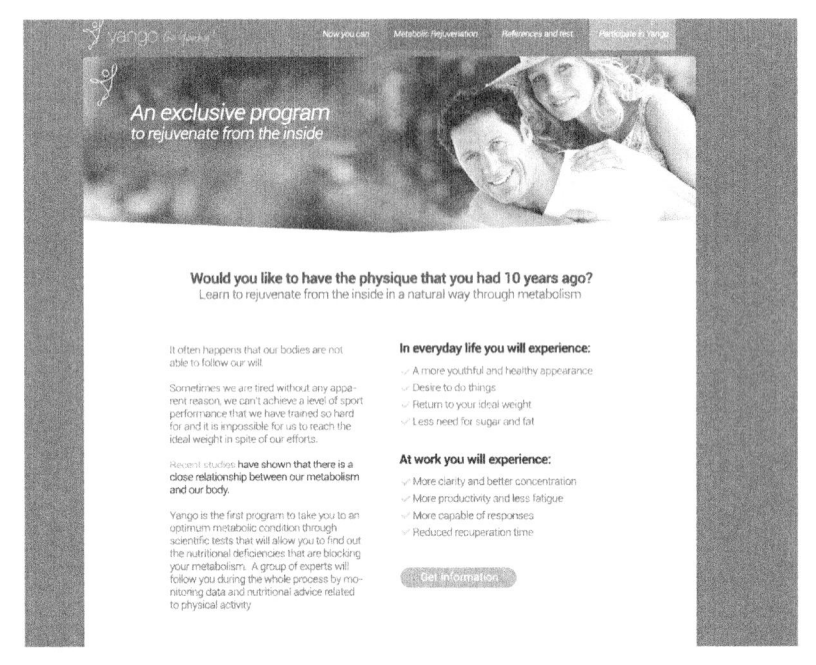

Image 3.5 – The mix of information on the Yango landing page

On the landing page done for the ad-on FoxContact, I faced a different but equally interesting challenge. FoxContact, as I explained in Chapter 1 is software that allows whoever has created a web with Joomla! to create simple and quick contact forms. It is an amazing component furthermore because apart from being easy to use, it is also flexible and is equipped with great functions for advanced users.

Who is it aimed at, then? Inexperienced users who want to create contact forms without going crazy, or expert users that need more advanced features, like for example, the follow-up of the contacts and the registration of the forms received?

We have aimed at everyone. Based on the assumption that anyone, expert or not, wants to work quickly and create forms without going crazy I have created a chart divided into two columns that shows, on the left side, the

3 – The rules of attraction | 119

main advantages for new users and on the right side those reserved for those who are more familiar with CMS. Whether you are an expert or a beginner at a glance you will be able to find all the information that you need (Image 3.6).

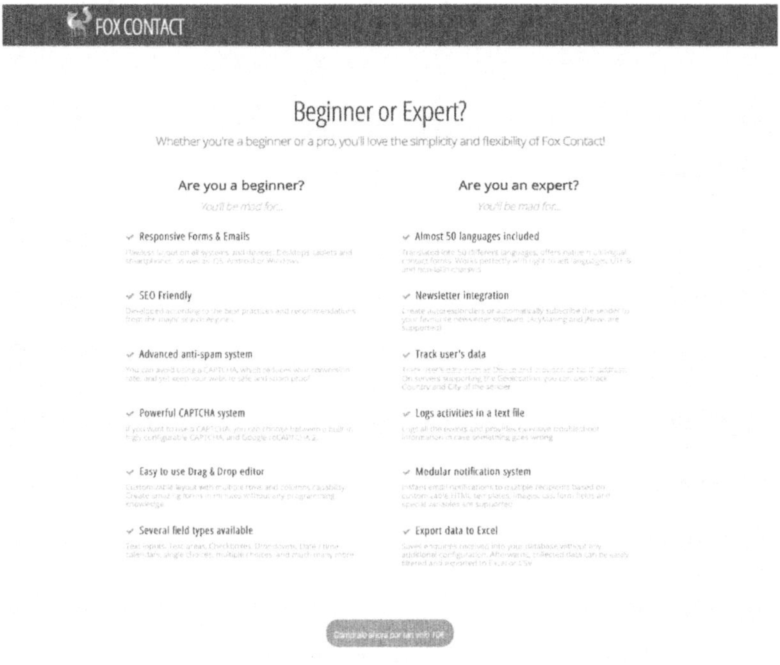

Image 3.6 – The FoxContact table of advantages differentiates the function advantages depending on the level of the user.

The landing phase

The first anchor.

At this point it could be useful to throw down a first anchor about the price. The anchor effect is a cognitive distortion that "keeps us anchored" to a value where there is no additional information available offering those who contact us or show interest in the price the possibility to play with the contrast between the initial and the real value. In practice, the anchor effect is the tendency of our brain to use any reference value as a starting point and comparison for successive valuations: for example, I could tell you that the cost of service X until recently was over 10,000$, but that now the prices, fortunately, are a little more accessible. I'm not telling you what it really costs at this moment, I'm just going to leave that concept in your head and move on, for example to testimonials or information that will allow me to justify the higher initial price.

If you continue to read the offer, you will understand and justify the high initial price (even if it doesn't fit your budget). At a later point in the offer, when the price has already been set in your brain at 10,000 $, you will discover that you only really need a budget of only 4000 $ today. At this point the actual price of the service, 4000 $, will seem much more advantageous than it would have seemed without making use of the anchor effect.

Among Daniel Kahneman's magic individualized cognitive distortions, anchoring is probably my favourite: combined with the principle of contrast[13], it allows us to create interesting effects.

If for example I have to design a landing page for an acceleration service for Apple laptops via the substitution of the fixed disc for an SSD, I could say:

> *"Thanks to the service of MACfaaast you will not have to pay 1799$ for a new iMac, bring your computer to us and you can pick it up 3 hours later".*

---

13. Cialdini Robert B., Influence: The Psychology of Persuasion, Harper Business, 2006.

I don't say the price. Not at this moment.
I create the anchor and proceed with the natural flow of my content.

While the user reads, the figure is fixed in his mind, and when he reaches the price of the service, it will be perceived as much more convenient because of anchoring effect and the rule of contrast. I have talked about the anchor effect at this point because it is at this point on the page, at the end of the section dedicated to interest that I generally set it in motion. But we will discover all the tricks about anchors, baits and contrast in the chapter dedicated to the rules of desire.

...The journey is going to be long and interesting!

ADVICE FROM THE AUTHOR

At this point at the end of each chapter I recommend that you take a break. If you have 15-20 minutes I suggest you go to the support page (https://landing-page-effectiveness.com/gym/) to put into practice the concepts set out and to better assimilate the information I have given you so far. All you will need is a simple sheet of paper, a black marker, a highlighter and a pen. With these exercises you can start to design your page, which you can develop as you read the book. Of course, it is not going to be the final one but it will be a great help to start translating these ideas into a design.

See you soon! https://landing-page-effectiveness.com/gym/

Takeaway

The landing phase: TODAY
In this phase we need to try and prevent the user from going back and leaving our page. The objective is that after reading the header they scroll down and click on the invitation to action.

❶ Identifying the problem

1. Identify a group of people with a specific problem and create a solution directed uniquely at them. You can analyse the product or service to extract the unique selling proposition, understanding what you can contribute by interviewing your clients or indeed developing a completely new offer, but it should always be the response to a problem or a concrete need in a niche of the market.

2. Go into the problem in depth in all its facets, speaking with people that are already your clients or could be your clients. You must empathise with them and get to know what they want, their doubts and their fears

3. Go back over the problem with a question, imitating as much as possible the terminology used by your clients. If the segment of clients that you want to reach need help to solve 'hunger pains' instead of 'hunger pangs' imitate their way of expressing: Are you looking for help to prevent hunger pains?

❷ The rules of attraction

1. Take care deeply with the header image. It has the task of highlighting, explaining and reinforcing the text that accompanies it. The image can (choose your option):
   a. show the object of the offer, possibly whilst it is being used;
   b. make the user project into the future, when they will have obtained the benefits;
   c. create a link with the professional that will offer the service.

2. Take a lot of care with the copywriting of the header. Speak with the user in a personal way, directly about his problem. Create or extract a promise trying to make it as unique and exclusive as possible. Create a headline which grabs attention but using the keywords with which you want to position yourself. The header should contain the following elements:

a) the problem, translated into a question or affirmation that captures attention;
b) the title, that is to say, the solution to the problem, the user's "salvation" (with the principal key word);
c) the promise /unique selling proposition, that is to say, a guarantee for the user and better still if it contains an uniqueness element;
d) the introduction to the call to action (if it's necessary);
e) principal call to action

To test whether you have worked well and optimised your copy, you can use the A/B test from Google Ads to find out the best way to enunciate the problem and the order of importance of advantages for the user.

3. Take care of the design, colours and typeface. You must highlight, explain and reinforce the text.
The graphics on the landing page should meet the following conditions:
a) define the reading areas making the important elements clear and distinguishable;
b) use a homogenous colour scheme with which the CTA can be highlighted thanks to the complementary use of colour
(I generally always avoid red and purple);
c) create an easy to read panel where the text is divided into small parts;
d) use a typeface which allows you to easily distinguish the most important things.

To check if you have worked well, you can use the 'Usabilityhub' five second test to see if a person understands your offer at a glance, without reading the texts.

The conversion phase

still present in the mind of the user, for example "what if it's a scam? "What if I lose my money as well as waste my time?"
We are going to construct trust piece by piece so that soon we can focus ourselves on the "rules of desire", that is to say, on all the actions available to us to motivate the user into immediate action putting pressure, for example, to the prices and time limited offers. We will make advantageous use of the anchor, the bait effect and social proof to lead our user to say yes without thinking twice whilst still paying attention to all those users who are not yet ready and who skip over the contact form without filling in the fields or hitting "send".

In this phase we will also bear in mind the aspect that very few people pay attention to: the quality of the lead. We can intervene on the copy to filter the number of leads received, keeping only the best ones or working backwards, establishing downsell to obtain at least the email addresses in all those cases where the entry barriers are too important.

We still have a lot to do! Let's not waste time! Let's get to work!

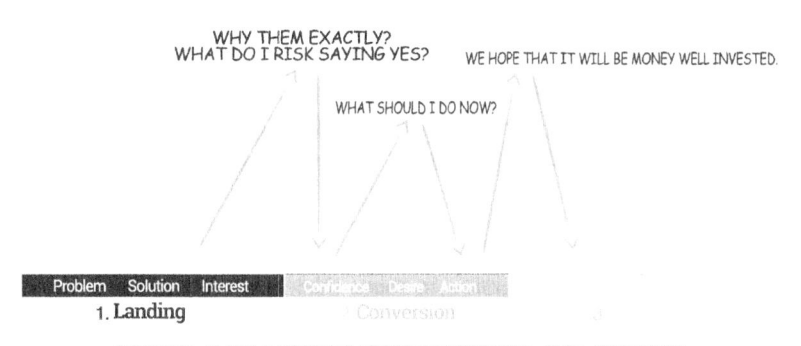

TODAY THE WINNER IS YOU

The conversion is illustrated from the perspective of the method TODAY the WINNER is YOU

Chapter 4
FORGING TRUST

What are we talking about here?
Being able to convince users that they need to put themselves in contact with us we need to reduce the feeling of risk; the fear of losing is stronger than the desire to obtain. To reassure them with need to use all strategies available, implementing them in the best manner, one after the other.

Even if you have created a fantastic offer you shouldn't forget that up until now the only person that has spoken about it and praised its advantages is yourself.

Rarely does anyone publicly admit the disadvantages of their offer and it is easy to make it seem that "everything is beautiful and convenient", but will this be true? One of the most common mistakes in creating commercial offers is not including a risk reversal section in which we can eliminate all possible risks for our potential client. No matter what you sell, even if it is free, you are always going to have a certain level of resistance that will push your user to let go or postpone the decision.

In order of importance these elements are:

1. Video feedback;
2. Photo of the client;
3. Link to social profile of the client;
4. Name, surname, position in the company and city;
5. The name of his company;
6. Date of purchase of the service or product.

Apart from the video which is very difficult to get, the photo is a good starting point to create credibility. If we get a photo of the customer using the product, the feedback will be even more effective.

> **WHERE SHOULD WE UPLOAD THE TESTIMONIAL VIDEOS?**
>
> If you use videos, I advise you to upload them to YouTube, where you can insert your company logo in the channel settings, which will appear in the video. When you insert the video in the page, use the web http://embedresponsively.com to avoid that the iframe spoils the visualization in mobile devices.

After the videos and photos, in order of importance, we will find the client's name and surname and all the information that demonstrates that it is indeed a real person. In the example in the image 4.2, the Invincible Offer, developed for an evening conversation course, I put the comments in a beautiful 3x3 frame from which you can access the well-made videos, where clients speak about their experiences in the English school Intensive Business English.

The photo is really important and often constitutes the boundary between an effective reference and one that will have little impact on the person reading it: we need to see people and above all, know that they are like us and that we can trust them.

4 - Forging trust | 135

Why should I register right now?
Some words from those that participated in the course

"Class with few people that allowed me to interact"
Fabio Dieni – Employed

"Good group, good teacher and topics which are going to help me get better"
Alessandra Micelli – Personal Assistant

"My focus has improved and I have more confidence"
Ilario Pedrini – Employed

"I liked the location, the price and the number of participants in the class"
Gabriel Serna – Employed

"Availability and possibility to practise dialogue"
Valentina Mango – Student

"Good value for money with a suitable method for the objectives"
Claudio Lorenzo Conti – Employed

"I felt very comfortable. Excellent timetable and pricing"
Serena Meraviglia – Pensioner

"Small groups and mid-term evaluation tests"
Alessandro Imbrenda – Employed

"Clear and transparent offer, excellent quality-price ratio"
Eleonora Adriani – Student

Image 4.2 - If you want to make the testimony not necessarily linked to the video, below I have introduced a part of the client's comment, followed by name, surname and profession (www.conversazione-ininglese.it). In this way, whoever reads the page knows the content of the video even without hitting play.

For this reason, targeting a specific market segment is always a good idea. In the comments about the evening conversation course in English, 8 out of the 9 references are from people between the ages of 25 and 40 who work during the day and are exactly the landing page's target. This is because we tend to trust those who are more like us and belong to our social group: this "resemblance" between the one who leaves the commentary and the one who reads it also makes it more effective.

Unfortunately, we also have to fight against the fact that not everyone wants to appear in a photo, especially when it comes to large companies. If our referee does not want to be exposed in the first person, we can put the name of the company and the date of acquisition of the product to start publishing the comments while waiting for more complete references. Anonymity makes the comment impersonal and that is not good; therefore, we can start filling the page, but we will have to replace these references.

The main problem in any case is to get the first references. When you have 12-15 willing participants almost nobody will mind appearing because they will see that others have already agreed to do it.

Do everything possible to get the first reviews

Do everything you need to get the first feedback, everything is appropriate, as when we go deeper into the funnel part related to the extended satisfaction, you will be greatly assisted by this process and everything will be made easier.

Something very useful on a visual level are the little **stars**.
In a recent study tests were carried out on how users read references on websites. They revealed that most of the users "scan" them quickly, paying more attention to the total ratings and the stars than to the text itself. Consequently, it seems that it is better to publish 8 short five-star comments than 2 longer five-star references.

4 - Forging trust 137

I believe it also depends on the type of website you look at and at how many comments are posted, how reliable they are considered and how hard the user searches. Personally, I have not done much testing on this, but from experience I think the reference should be long enough to tell an experience with which the reader can identify with immediately.

Do users read web pages quickly? I talked about it in a recent speech, publishing a single slide that shows some Google Analytics data extracted from a Landing Page of mine (Image 4.3), specifically:

- 21 minutes of permanence for those that browse from a laptop or PC;
- 6 minutes of permanence for those that browse from a smartphone;
- 4 minutes of permanence for those that browse from a tablet.

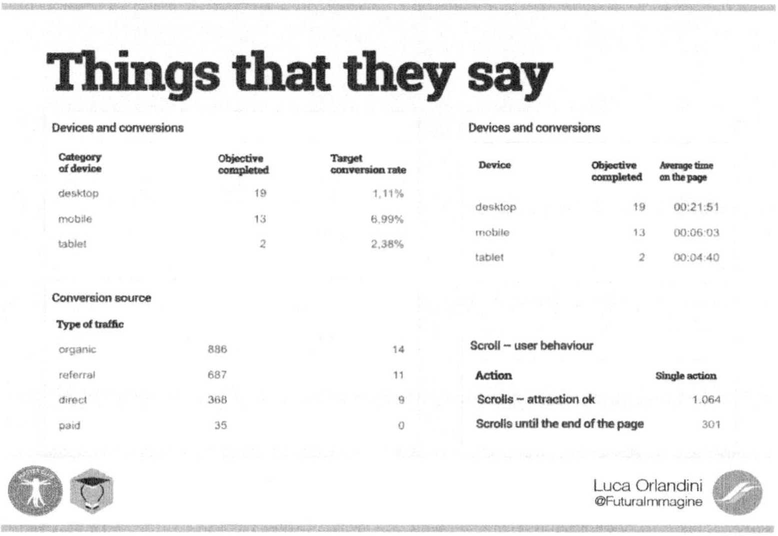

Things that they say

Devices and conversions

Category of device	Objective completed	Target conversion rate
desktop	19	1.11%
mobile	13	6.99%
tablet	2	2.38%

Conversion source

Type of traffic

organic	886	14
referral	687	11
direct	368	9
paid	35	0

Devices and conversions

Device	Objective completed	Average time on the page
desktop	19	00:21:51
mobile	13	00:06:03
tablet	2	00:04:40

Scroll – user behaviour

Action	Single action
Scrolls – attraction ok	1.064
Scrolls until the end of the page	301

Luca Orlandini
@FuturaImmagine

Image 4.3 – A slide taken from the speech. Look at the time spent on an effective landing page: it doesn't seem that people are in a hurry to "read" the page!

If we create an effective design and encourage the reading of our content users will stop at our site. This evidence however, does not make the little stars a secondary element: they allow us at a glance to get an idea of the opinions without reading them. People will read the text if the words are appropriate and if the comments are interesting and credible.

> *The most common expression you hear about advertising is that people will not read much. Yet a vast amount of the best-paying adverting shows that people do read much.*
> Claude Hopkins

Try to get effective references: in my experience, two lines are almost never enough to express an opinion that goes beyond the superficial. What really convinces are stories and real experiences, especially if they are well told.

As I said in the introduction, the reference shouldn't only achieve the function of a positive testimonial, but also reduces any possible objection that might exist in the mind of the person that reads it.

The more references that we have, the more possibilities we have to reduce doubts in user's mind. Whoever reads the reference should know that other people also had doubts at the beginning, that it is normal but they were able to overcome them and that their action has led them to the solution to their problem and satisfaction. By using references in this way you are able to reduce possible perceived risks and generate desire.

We will go into more depth into the best way to collect the references in the chapter dedicated to the collection of feedbacks in the section dedicated to satisfaction.

Not only positive reviews

References are a fantastic conversion tool so I advise you to dedicate the necessary time to them and to publish not only those that are really positive, but also those that are more articulate and that list some of the setbacks which were later solved during the course of the project.

On my webpage I published a client review who complained a little because the landing page needed more time than expected to generate contacts, but in the end he recognised that he was satisfied because he had increased the number of courses he organized each month.

Don't only put 5 star reviews, also put those of 4 or 3 stars.

Rossella Cenini, a friend of mine, in her Blog put forward an interesting question: if we are sure that we shouldn't only publish 5 star reviews, then where should we place the 3-4 stars? Is it better to place them at the beginning or at the end of the area dedicated to references?

The objective is to put these opinions in there but that in the flow of reading they are not fixed in our memory, giving precedence to those that are completely positive.

To try to answer this question, let's look at two very interesting and contrasting cognitive distortions known as the "primacy" effect and the "recency" effect.

The primacy effect is immediate and subconscious and leads us to fix the first impression in the brain, creating an inevitable conditioning effect on all our future assessments.

When Oscar Wilde affirmed that "you won't have a second chance to make a good first impression", he was referring precisely to this cognitive distortion. The primacy effect is a mental process that leads you to categorise one thing in a particular box in your head.

If you have formed a first impression about something it is true that you can modify it but only with a certain voluntary effort: the information that follows with the assistance of the primacy effect will inevitably be conditioned and distorted by this initial vision.

So, you might consider "creative" a person who is actually simply "disorganized", subconsciously creating automatic justifications that confirm your first impression: we are naturally inclined to be consistent with our ideas, even when they are based on a fleeting first impression.
So, all you have to do is post the best comments first? No, that'd be too easy. There is also the recency effect, which works the other way around. As a result of this cognitive distortion, the last piece of information acquired (imagine the final part of a speech) becomes more easily accessible, and therefore, a priority.

I know that now you feel a little bit confused and it is understandable. Which of the two effects is stronger? In a debate is it better to speak first or last?

These two focusses seem to drive us to contradictory conclusions, but this doesn't mean that the order of presentation doesn't have any importance and neither does it mean that it is impossible to make a reliable prediction: knowing the functioning of both processes, we can predict in which circumstances the primacy effect predominates and in which on the contrary the recency effect predominates.

A fundamental variable is the time interval between the different phases.

If the public has to make a decision **IMMEDIATELY AFTER** the speech, the recency effect will predominate, while if the decision is made in the future, the primacy effect will be more important until it is the only one considered[15].

This is because the primacy effect involves long-term memory whilst the recency effect takes advantage of the speed with which we can obtain information from our short-term memory [16].

---

15. Aronson Elliot, *The Social Animal*, Worth/Freeman, 2011.
16. Motterlini Matteo, Trappole mentali: Come difendersi dalle proprie illusioni e dagli inganni altrui, BUR, 2010.

As far as reviews are concerned, the solution is simpler: the publishing base should be where you place the neutral or less enthusiastic opinions at the centre of the reference block, interspersed with more positive reviews. They will make the section look more credible and will be assimilated without our reader being able to attribute much weight to them.

How many references to publish and where

Normally, in my offers I publish blocks where at least 4 opinions are seen at the same time and if I can I'll even use 6-8. With the reviews I usually dedicate a vertical space of about 2000 pixels (to avoid the situation where a user who wants to skip them must do a lot of scrolling), but if I can publish more, I will always do so keeping them hidden and loading them through a special button.

Watch out: the new reviews shouldn't substitute those that are already published but should add to those that are already on the page. The general appearance is always very important and for that reason a slideshow (or carousel) is a bad idea either to display reviews or for any other content.

> *Reviews are fundamental and are one of the elements*
> *least taken advantage of in commercial offers.*
> *A single well-written review together with a good call to action*
> *can constitute a winning sales letter.*

On my landing pages I publish the reviews in the area of the creation of trust, but when I can I also repeat some just after the area dedicated to the call to action which I have called "desire after action". This trick works because users who go beyond the area of action do so in search of a little extra motivation or because they still have some doubts that can be solved by a well-written review.

Satisfied or refund

There are several actions we can take to reduce the risk to our potential customers. The basic idea is that in your offer there is EVERYTHING to win and NOTHING to lose.

To obtain this result we can offer diverse guarantees or conditions that progressively increase the insurance of our potential client, but always considering that this type of action, although very effective, can involve a small risk that must be calculated in our lead optimisation phase.

Progressively, we can achieve a risk conversion by measuring:

- "Satisfied or refund" guarantee for 30 days sometimes obligatory by law;
- "Satisfied or refund" for a prolonged period of time;
- "Satisfaction or refund" guarantee with an "easy return" policy including the coverage of shipping costs (for example in zappos.com);
- "Satisfied or refund" guarantee with 200% amount returned.

In Italy the first level, also called the "right of withdrawal", provides for the possibility of returning the product within 30 days with a full refund. This level of security is dictated by law in most countries (for online or telephone purchases) and in Italy it is accompanied by the following restrictions:

1. may be exercised only in relation to contracts for the sale of goods or services done remotely or outside the physical establishment;
2. may be exercised only in relationship between a seller and a consumer (understood as a person acting for non-business purposes) and only by the latter in relation to the former;
3. can be exercised by the consumer without obligation to give explanations about the causes or motivations that led him to dissolve the contract;
4. MUST be communicated by the seller, who is obliged to inform the

consumer about this possibility.

The right of withdrawal is inalienable and cannot be subject to penal sanctions or restrictions and each contractual clause that limits it is considered null and void.

In some types of sale the right of withdrawal is excluded but in a lot of others it is sanctionable by law. If your service or product provides for a right of withdrawal, the first thing you should do is to communicate it effectively. You must ALWAYS communicate it by law, so it is worth giving the message as if it were your own choice motivated by the trust you give to your product or service.

Can you remember how they present the right of withdrawal in telesales? In this way, you will have the possibility to transform a threat (you have to refund someone) into an opportunity (convince more clients). If your product is among those with a right of withdrawal then you are on a same level with your competitors and the only strong point may be to communicate this possibility effectively.

Or you can do more. You could extend the deadline for requesting a refund or the value you will return by going BEYOND your product. In addition to paying the cost of the product to be refunded, you could, for example, even assume the cost of shipping the goods to and from the consumer. Or you can do as the direct marketing experts Bencivenga and Rosenthal who in a famous advertisement said:

> "We guarantee that we can beat your best ad by at least 10% or you will not pay for our work. Test us and if we don't come out as the winner, not only will we not insist on payment, but we will reimburse you for all the expenses outlaid in having tested us.
> Did you use the Wall Street Journal to test our advert and invested $10,000? Well, if we don't win, we'll reimburse you.
> We're only doing this because we're confident of winning."

In this case we are obviously not talking about client satisfaction but achieving an outcome. The small inherent trick in this offer is measuring the advertising results in a scientific way which in those years was very difficult (even today where it is very simple, many entrepreneurs do not measure their ROI in web marketing so imagine what it was like in the 1960's). That said, we are talking about two authentic legends whose copywriting formulas really were capable of beating any advertisement of that time.

When we speak of the "satisfaction or refund" guarantee to amplify the effect of our guarantee we can do this using the disassembling technique by means of this cognitive distortion to affirm:

▶ "You can return the shoes bought in our online shop for any reason and we even pay for the courier",

This is not as effective as saying:

▶ "Have you chosen the wrong size? Do you not like the colour? Do you think there was another model that would have suited you better? You can return them and we will pay the courier".

Citing Motterlini in his Mental Traps: "the disassembling principle provides that the estimated probability associated with the description of a state of affairs will tend to increase if that state is described in more detail, making explicit possibilities that would otherwise be implicit"[22]

When you use the formula "satisfaction or refund" you expose yourself to the risk that someone may be reimbursed but at the same time you also attract a lot of people who were waiting for their last fear to be eliminated.

It is true that we all fear the people that will take advantage of this clause and are going to ask for a refund even if the service of product is perfect but these exceptions actually fall under a calculated and acceptable risk: the percentage of refunds is statistically low and is largely exceeded by the increase in orders generated by the announcement.
To protect themselves from these same clauses businesses place limits

---

22. Motterlini Matteo, Trappole mentali: Come difendersi dalle proprie illusioni e dagli inganni altrui, BUR, 2010 (Mental traps: how to defend yourself from your own illusions and from others decivings).

4 - Forging trust

making it more difficult to request a refund or defining the conditions you have to satisfy in order to qualify for it.

Personally, I think the best way is to always give a response to this type of claim. A dissatisfied client can do a lot more economical damage than a small refund, whilst if they are also satisfied, they can speak well of the service to other clients even if their experience with the product wasn't positive. Customer service ALWAYS plays a key role in these events so make sure that whoever performs this delicate task has the appropriate sensitivity to their function.

The last but not least important factor.

Whatever your profession or job you can refuse to work on a project that you do not consider suitable for your service or with a customer who seems problematic.
Sometimes I had to deal with entrepreneurs who wanted to promote products or services that didn't meet the fundamental requirements for success in the market.

In these cases, even if I don't sell a service with the "satisfied of refunded" clause, I clearly explain that unfortunately I cannot help them and the most of the times I reject the project. Since my time is limited, I must concentrate on projects with higher probability of success.

But, I'm selling a service.

If instead, I could make economies of scale for example by selling a premade product, my tolerance limit would clearly be different, and I would adopt a different and less selective strategy.

Going back to the type of warranty, keep in mind that there are infinite variations which can be experienced and tested over time: you can find

> **AUTHOR'S ADVICE**
>
> If you are a consultant, I advise you that over time and at my expense, I have learned that knowing how to choose one's clients and projects is a very important quality for those who do our work. We really have a lot of work to do and a lot of things to study (either to keep up to date or to increase our skills), and we can't waste energy in unprofitable or even uneconomic ancillary activities.

a lot of articles or template about this with a simple search on Google. Is there anything more powerful and effective than warranty forms? Of course there is: the free trial. We will learn to appreciate it and take advantage of it in our favour in the following section.

"Free trial"

The next and most effective level is to facilitate the testing of the service. I have placed the term "free" in quotes because those who agree to try our service for free actually pay us in a way: they choose our service over that of the competition.

Often the main obstacle is inertia; "breaking the ice" and starting a collaborative relationship with someone, even if it is for free, increases the chances that a more solid paying relationship will be created in the future.

Most of the company's main objective is the creation of a relationship and secondly the monetisation of the relationship.

Think about the low cost offers that you find in fast food restaurants where, with only a few $, you can buy a baguette roll and chips. The objective is that you feel as if you are in their place, creating a relationship and establishing habits.

Today it also works a lot in training: if a training day with a professional costs 1000 $, low-cost tickets are put together that are simply "sales letters" where it is possible to access the course with payments that have the sole purpose of covering the fixed costs of room and equipment. During the promotion the contents will be transmitted but nothing really important: the most evident message will be that you need to sign up to the seminar costing 3000 $ to really achieve the objectives.

The objective is to build a relationship over time that is not based on a single sale but on many sales of a value that grow progressively over time.

It is the so-called "foot in the door" technique, which consists of convincing someone to do something by means of a small request.

FIRST YES
    "Hello, are you in favour of mothers that work?"
    "Of course I am, why not?"
    "Would you sign up? It only takes 5 seconds and it is important for people to see that in 2022 it is indispensable for the professional career of a woman to be compatible with the desire to have children".
    "I'm in a bit of a hurry, but ok, where do I sign?"

SECOND YES
    "Here, look, take my pen... thank you very much, John, it's great to find people like yourself. I've been here all morning getting cold
and I really needed your help. We wanted to get a small room with a stove, but the association has no funds..."
    "Don't worry, it has been a pleasure!"
    "Would you also like to help our association?
It costs less than a Euro per day..."

...BINGO!

It is for this reason that most people in Milan who are stopped in the street reject everything. The principal problem in these techniques is that they use patterns. Our brains are biologically constructed to identify them and as soon as they know how this technique works it's easy to recognise it. For this reason we need to be a little creative and shouldn't carry out these learnt notions to the letter but adapt them to distinct contexts.

Returning to ourselves, offering a free trial or a discount is a good idea. I also use a system to reduce the initial amount of force and the perceived risk of those that want to commission me an Invincible Offer. If you have a business idea but you are not sure if it is going to work or you simply need some strategic advice before you invest you can get my consultant start-up package. You can obtain up to 4 hours of consultancy at 50% of the normal price and if you decide to develop a landing page the cost of these hours already expended are reimbursable.

In this way my potential clients can obtain direct feedback about their project, practical advice and ideas about prioritising actions, but above all they can get to know me and see that their project is suitable for the internet and I am the person that they have been looking for.

> *The advantage of the free trial is that it allows us to ensure that our user makes a choice that, if we are suitable and meet their expectations, will be confirmed over time. For the principle of consistency, as pointed out by Robert Cialdini, we tend to confirm our choices by continuing on the path we have taken, just as a body in motion tends to maintain its state of movement.*

Other services provide a free trial of 30 days (Image 4.4), and again, the difference is in the barriers to entry which in order of commitment require:

- name, surname, email;
- name, surname, email and answer some questions (you will be included in the email marketing systems);

4 - Forging trust 149

- credit card on which nothing will be charged. You will have to confirm the activation of the service (explicit activation)
- credit card on which at the end of the free trial, the cost of the service will be charged (implicit activation)

Image 4.4 - GetResponse has one of the most beautiful and effective communication styles you can find online. It offers a free trial for 30 days, even without a credit card.

Which is the best solution? Each case is unique and tests would be necessary but the most important thing is to know that people tend to maintain their status quo and as a consequence such a system with automatic renewal can invoice thousands of Euros thanks to people who do not feel like cancelling or forget to do so when the time comes.

Our objective is very important: if we have just launched a new service it could be convenient to have many "active" clients so as to be able to publish their number; in this case I would choose to apply the card stipulation only at the end of the trial period to favour more accounts being opened.

If, on the contrary, my service is already up and running and well known it could be useful to ask for data immediately so that the subscription is done automatically and the action that the user must take is to block our invoice to make it not possible (the user will always tend not to react). Most of the times we go back to the status quo even for things much more important than a simple subscription to an online service.

In some European countries the percentage of people that have signed up to organ donation is 95% whilst in some others they fight to achieve more than 10%. If the cultural context is similar how can such a difference be justified in such an important and decisive aspect of daily life? In the end a life can depend on a donation.

In both cases to show one's willingness to donate organs you only have to sign a document but the substantial difference is the default option; in countries with 95% consent rate it is necessary to act in order to NOT be a donor (one is a default donor), while in countries with 90% NO donors it is necessary to act in order to be one.

It's the power of inertia.

Resist the dark side, use the "default option" wisely

As we have seen most people tend not to adjust the default option and this feature can be used to our advantage, but there is also something very important to keep in mind: every sale, in the TODAY the WINNER is YOU process, is based on a relationship of trust which allows us to build value over time.

Everything we do to accompany our users towards conversion should NEVER seem like something obligatory or framed in a way as removing their freedom of choice.

4 – Forging trust 151

We should make their decision seem natural and we dont' have to force them or make them take decisions before they are really ready.

A user who feels forced to do something will not buy and worse still, someone who feels manipulated will speak badly of you. The final objective is always satisfaction that should go beyond their expectations (we'll talk about this in a separate chapter).

I saw in first person an example of how you shouldn't use the default option on a web site where I buy stock images for my projects. In these enormous archives you can buy images or illustrations which are free of royalties by credit and subscription: the credits don't have an expiry date and are priced according to resolution whilst the subscription allows you to download a certain amount of images in a certain amount of time, for example, one month, after which you won't have further access.

The cost of downloading an image via subscription is 10-15 times less than buying it with credits. Downloading two images a while ago made me realise at my expenses that the default option, even if you have an active subscription intends credits to be used. As I didn't change the option (I was in a hurry and didn't look properly at the small drop-down menu) I paid 24 credits, which is the equivalent to more than 30 Euros for two images which I could have paid less than 1 Euro per unit.

Why has this page been designed this way? Is there really someone who would download images paying for their face value with credits that do not expire, when they have the possibility to download the same image with the same amount available every day which is lost when they don't use it up? I don't think so.

The problem is obviously not 30 Euros but the fact that the service made me feel stupid and duped. This bothered me so much that I contacted customer service – something I never do – to ask for a refund but was instead given 3 extra downloads without expiry.

Clearly, even if I had got my money back, their actual economic balance, bearing in mind the number of users who make mistakes and do not ask for a refund, would be positive. But I didn't get a refund: I got three free images. I was very unhappy. The perceived value of these three images for me was the same as 3 of the 80 images I still had for the rest of the month. What the hell I will do with other three images? Regardless of the incorrect approach and the unwillingness to placate me, the operator had made a mistake.

In reality this is about a communication problem and the way in which I was "sold" the refund. It would probably have been enough to know that these three images, since they do not expire, are actually worth 36 credits. I mistakenly spent 24 credits for which I not only got a refund but also received extra credit. They could have told me:

"I'm sorry for what has happened and of course we will refund you 24 credits. To further compensate you for your trouble, we are going to give you an additional 50% value, offering you a total refund of 36 credits.
It is important to us that you are happy. Unfortunately, however, I cannot recharge the credit because it is linked to our billing system and it is very complicated... but we see that you work a lot with us, so we will give you 3 images (each with a value of 12 credits) that you can choose from our catalogue. Also, unlike the credits that have an annual value, you can download these three images without time limit whilst we are operating in the market".

From this story I learnt two very important things that I would like to pass on to you:

- the default option should be used to facilitate the user's choice, not mislead them;
- the way we communicate a message is always relevant to the content.

4 - Forging trust   153

Use the default option whenever you can, but only to bring your client closer, not to get extra or inappropriate payments. If we fall victim to the dark side and make it difficult for the user to act on their decisions, the "devilish" design of our website will end up working against us.

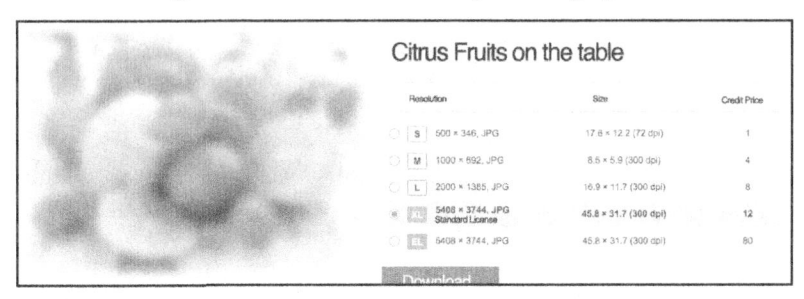

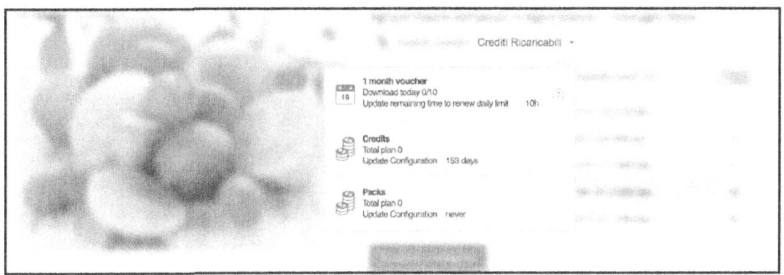

Imges 4.5 and 4.6 – The screen of the royalty free photos website where you can choose the payment method of the photo you want to download. The option is clear but the default option is the best for the seller, not for the user.

You probably think that this is just a detail and that I'm looking at it in more detail than a normal programmer would, but this is not the case. These devilishly designed systems are driving us. Do you want another proof?

My 30 day plan has come to an end and I find myself in a new charge. What happened? Is it a mistake?

154 | The conversion phase

No, the monthly subscription renewal is automatic and the way the sales process is managed makes it difficult to realise that. Or it tells you clearly, but does not give you the possibility to set the option to block the renewal of the purchase and makes it very difficult to find that setting in the account settings. More than once, with a well-known keyword analysis service, I have had to contact support via chat to be guided to deactivate the account. Is it a bad web design? No, it was simply designed with a specific objective: to make you pay at least one additional renewal.

The stock photo web that I had the problem with the credits also used this same technique, as you can see in Images 4.7 and 4.8.

Does it work in terms of profit? Yes.
Does it work in terms of business? Not if you want to create a lasting relationship.

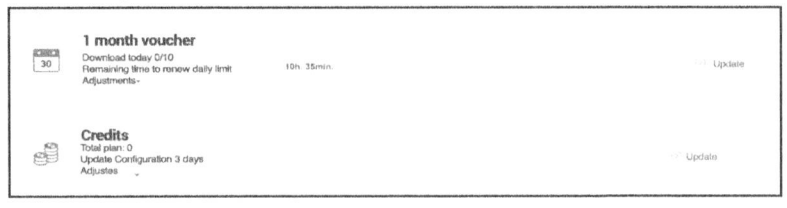

```
1 month voucher
Download today 0/10
30  Remaining time to renew daily limit   10h 35min.                    Update
    Adjustments-

    Credits
    Total plan: 0
    Update Configuration 3 days                                         Update
    Adjustes
```

Image 4.7 - The hidden option: in the image you can see in detail the page dedicated to the user and their existing contracts. How? Can't you see the option which lets you know about automatic renewal and which allows you to deactivate it? That's normal, it's hidden.

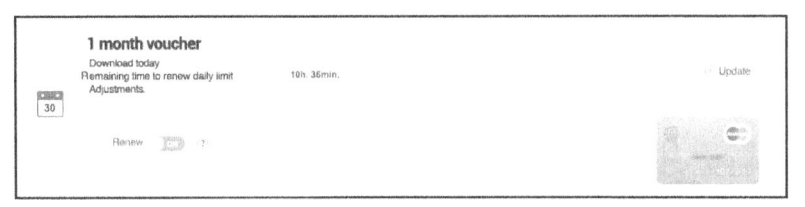

```
1 month voucher
Download today
Remaining time to renew daily limit   10h 36min.                        Update
30  Adjustments.

          Renew
```

Image 4.8 - The revealed option: When you click on "Configuration" this screen appears. As you can easily see, there aren't any configuration options, or additional information, just a simple "switch" that the company could have clearly shown on the previous screen.

ADVICE FROM THE AUTHOR

At this point at the end of each chapter I recommend that you take a break. If you have 15-20 minutes I suggest you go to the support page (https://landing-page-effectiveness.com/gym/) to put into practice the concepts set out and to better assimilate the information I have given you so far. All you will need is a simple sheet of paper, a black marker, a highlighter and a pen. With these exercises you can start to design your page, which you can develop as you read the book. Of course, it is not going to be the final one but it will be a great help to start translating these ideas into a design.

See you soon! https://landing-page-effectiveness.com/gym/

Chapter 5

THE RULES OF DESIRE

> **What are we talking about here?**
> How can we turn the fear of losing into an advantage in our favour?
> How can we convince those that have come this far to act immediately?

With our Invincible Offer! We have attracted the users' attention by capturing their need, progressively creating interest and eliminating their possible objections and perceived risks.

If we have done it well, our user will now be convinced that they have found what they were looking for and that we are the best solution for them. Probably they have already decided to contact us but they still needs a little push.

The time has finally come to publish the most requested information by those who are looking for information about a product or a service: the price. If, because of WYSIATI, this factor was reduced to being the only factor to be taken into account, it is essential that the user followed a formative path before being introduced to it.

Our user is finally prepared to find out the price of our service or product. Which is the best way to present it?

We have already planted the first seed: at the end of the section "TODAY" we published a mini-chapter dedicated to the anchor which prepared the user by indicating a much higher figure than that which will be found in this chapter. Thanks to the contrast now our price will seem much more accessible.

But not only this. To this more accessible price we will apply distinct techniques, for example a time-limited discount, that the amount will be lowered even further until our offer is truly irresistible.

The reason is that we should motivate our users to act immediately. It is not enough that they tell us that our service is interesting if afterwards they choose another one. We can't live on likes alone!

But anchorage, contrast, social proof, bait effect and the reduction of options are just some of the techniques we will see. It will be a bit more complex because we will have to deal with the numbers so I advise you to read this chapter at a time when you can pay maximum attention to it.

Shall we start?

How do we use the bait (and link the anchor)

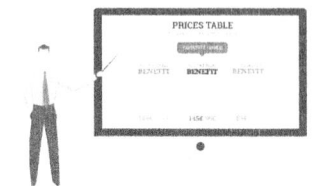

Do you remember in the interest phase when I told you about MACfaaast and how we dropped the anchor, talking about the price the user could avoid paying thanks to our SSD service?

This can be analysed here as well at the beginning of the area dedicated to the "rules of desire".

> "Thanks to Macfaaast you don't have to pay 1.799 Euros for a new iMac, bring us your computer and then pick it up 3 hours later."

5 – The rules of desire

We can now finally publish our prices which, compared with the price of 1.799 Euros of buying a new computer, can be very advantageous. The anchor sets you a reference value and taking advantage of the principle of contrast, manages to make you perceive the prices as more interesting and accessible. We can see it here (Image 5.1)

Image 5.1 - Price table for MACfaaast.it

Thanks to this table we can take advantage of the contrast in price of 1799 Euros for a new Mac and the substitution of the hard drive for a 1000 GB SSD, not to mention the contrast between the initial 1799 euros and the 199 euros for the most economical solution.

But we haven't finished yet and there is still a lot of work to be done on this table, because most users get stuck when they are faced with several similar options.

Western consumer culture has led us to think that having a lot of options is a good thing since it allows us to be the masters of our destiny. But in reality, our brain works in a different way. Choosing one option means giving up on all the others and with the increase in the number of options the chances of being wrong also increase. There is nothing that prohibits action as much as the possibility of being wrong.

For this reason, when they ask me: "Maybe it would have been better to suggest 10 SSD models?", or "Would it have been useful to give a choice between different brands of SSD?".

My response is always the same. No, the options are more than sufficient and we would have only run the risk of reducing the number of enquiries because of those insecure users that would have continued searching on the net so to have not made mistakes and then afterward resisted from buying. "Death or Glory" as said by The Clash: conversion or death. They have to choose now.

To help them choose, the most ideal is to guide them in their choice and reduce the number of available options thanks to the bait effect.

The bait effect provides for the creation of an unbalanced price table to encourage the purchase of a particular product, transforming one of the options into something advantageous (Image 5.2)[23].

In this table, as you can see, I have increased the price of the 500 GB disks to 449 Euros. The 1000 ones now cost only 50 Euros more and are also faster at 335% compared to 295%. In this situation few people buy the 500 one because the 1000 one is obviously perceived as much more convenient. Buying a new Mac will cost me 1799 Euros, a 1000 hard drive is practically a third of the cost and furthermore I am a professional so the 250 for domestic use isn't for me.

If during the landing on the page the motive was TO EXCITE, now we should work with the logic that whoever has been captured by our message (and has already chosen us) can reasonably justify his decision.

We have already gained something but we can still improve some things: an instrument is a little out of tune in the symphony.

The text saying "ONLY A FEW UNITS AVAILABLE" could, of course, make people think by looking at this table that the majority of people choose the most economical solution. Maybe the 1000 GB cost less

---

23. consider that this price table and the following ones, inserted in this section dedicated to bait effect, have been created for educational purposes.

5 – The rules of desire   161

because they are defective.
We can resolve this immediately with a small modification (Images 5.3).

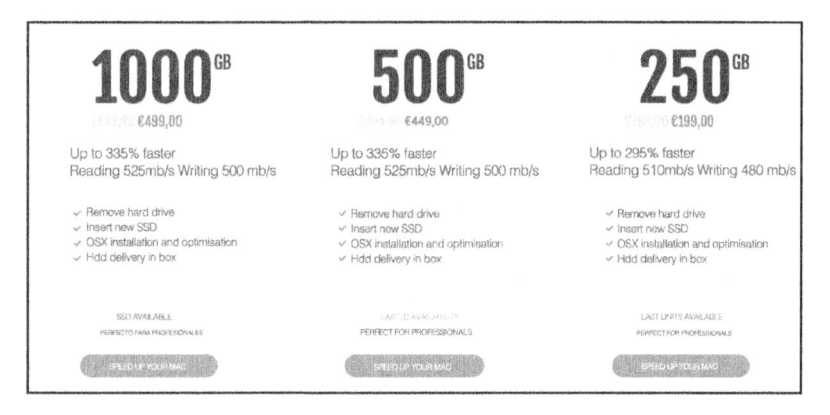

Image 5.2 – 499 euro or 449 euro?

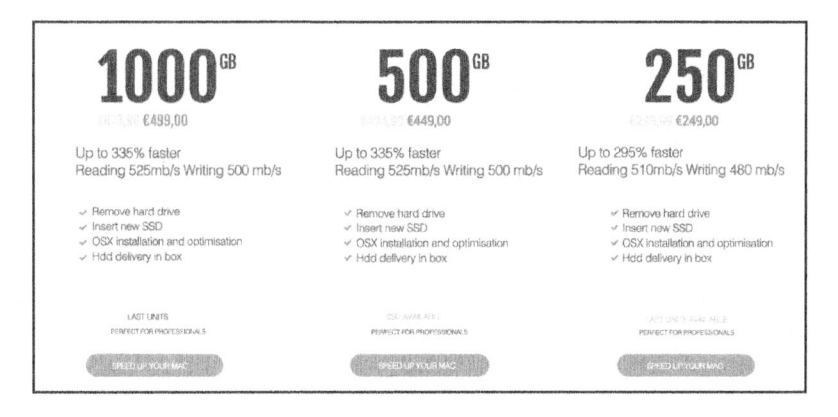

Image 5.3 – very few prices at 499 Euros vs 449 Euros..

162 The conversion phase

Here we are. The most sold solutions are those of 1000 or 250. Users are now correctly guided towards the choice we are most interested in or towards the option we want to make those who do not have enough budget fall into.

Later on we can make things better (Image 5.4) writing below the 250 "31 UNITS AVAILABLE" (in orange in the original), and below that of 1000 "13 UNITS AVAILABLE" (in red in the original). Indicating precise figures actually increases the perception of scarcity and helps to make our message more credible.

At this point our table is optimised and helps the user to choose between the available options, whether that be 1000 GB or 250 GB.

If instead of having two products to tempt the user, we had only one, we could use this tactic to tempt the user towards the product in the centre of the table, as seen in image 5.5.

I reduce the differences between the two higher ranking products by making the 600 GB product perceived as "still too expensive" and at the same time bringing the price of the 250 GB product closer making it almost as expensive as the 500 GB product.

This technique is often used in the cinema when they offer us popcorn or Coca-Cola "super size" at 10 $ while the "big" one is sold at 5-6 $ and is only a little bit smaller.

If you find yourself facing these sorts of prices don't think "Come on, nobody is going to buy it at this price, option B is much more convenient!" Whoever has established the prices isn't stupid, they have helped you to choose because you need it.

Why are too many options a problem?

According to a study on saving done by Sheena Iyengar, Gur Huberman, Emir Kamenica and Wei Jiang, people "choose not to choose", although

5 – The rules of desire   163

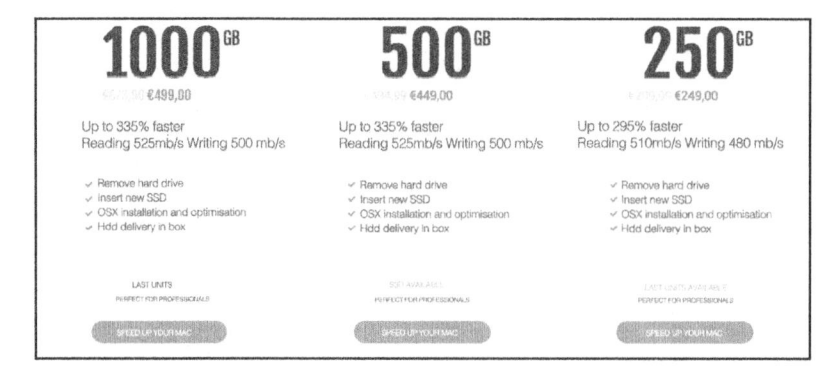

Image 5.4 - few pieces, specific numbers : 499 euro vs 449 euro

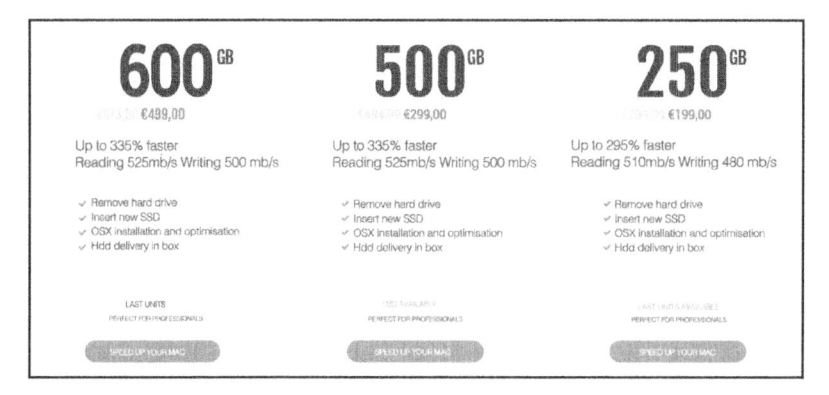

Image 5.5 - Few pieces and convenience for 500GB.
this actually goes against their own interests.

What motivates us is that, when faced with an endless number of options, we do not manage to perceive the differences and so we are trapped by the fear of making the wrong decision.

Sheena offers four techniques to avoid this deadlock which I illustrate briefly below.

▸ **Diminish the number of available options**
It has been proved scientifically that reducing similar or redundant

options leads to an increase in sales (as well as a reduction in costs). While it's true that Walmart, the market leader, offers a selection of more than 100 000 products, in ninth place among American retailers is Aldi which offers a selection of only 1400 products.

Define the consequences of each choice
In an experiment aimed at subscribing to an ING pension plan, a sample of people were asked how their lives would have changed if they had managed to save more money. This simple question, which the respondents had to answer in writing, increased the subscriptions in the group by 20%, as well as the amount of money allocated to the plan.

- **Use categories**
  We are better at managing descriptive categories than options. The important thing is that the subdivision by category has the objective of helping the buyer (not the seller) and therefore the difference is detectable and the shopping experience simplified.

- **Conditions of complexity**
  If we take for example the purchase of a car, we will have several issues that comprise a certain number of options. Some of the issues, such as colour, present 30 options, while others, such as exchange rate, only 4 options. Sheena has detected that starting with the issues that have fewer options and gradually increasing the level of complexity leads more users to complete the test. Starting with the simple options aids the user in learning how to choose (and perhaps because of the principle of consistency they then tend to continue with and complete the questionnaire).

If you are interested in this topic, when you have finished this chapter visit the support web Https://landing-page-effectiveness.com/dojo/. In the "resource" section you will find more videos from Sheena Iyengar and other useful presentations which study these theme in more depth.

The psychologist Barry Schwartz who specialises in the connection

5 – The rules of desire 165

between psychology and economy, has, in addition to having carried out a fun TED convention (which you can watch at http://bit.ly/barryted) has also published a book, The Paradox of Choice, of which I have also found an interesting video-resume in English (http://bit.ly/paradoxvid).

Helping to choose with social proof

To help our user with their selection we can also use tags with the inscription "recommended option" or "most popular option". The objective of these graphic elements is to guide whoever visits the offer towards the best choice (for us or for them) taking advantage of the principal of social

Image 5.6 - Best choice badge and highlighted prices.

proof, which, once more is highlighted by Robert Cialdini (Image 5.6). Social proof can be useful to confirm who reads a table of prices, what the users value and how they can choose a more precise offer, but there are even more useful and less evident techniques, for example the purchase of likes or other social signals.

What does it mean to buy a social signal? A lot of people say that it is stupid or useless to buy likes, but, like any tactical action, it can be effective if it is framed within the correct strategy.
Suppose that we need to create a landing page to sell guidance against

problems like premature ejaculation or eating disorders. Having a high number of "likes" will probably not be enough to push you towards purchasing but if the page that presents the offer is effective and the copy has been well-written, a high number of shares will mean that the person that reads the offer will feel less alone and provide them with an extra stimulus that can determine the acquisition or the rebound.

Likes, shares and visualisations (for YouTube videos) can be acquired by packets, like fruit at the market but generally I don't advise you to do it. They are a very accessory element to a page's efficiency and in order of preference there are other things that should be done first. It is true also that they can help and in certain contexts they make sense.

> *We will use the choices of others to define our best conduct the more similar to ourselves we find them*[24].
> Robert Cialdini

Social proof is fantastic offline as well as online and I'm not proud of being a victim of it; anyone that knows me knows that I always use two rules to choose a restaurant when I am in a city that I don't know:

1. The first is to be away from the centre and the tourist zone. There will probably be some excellent restaurants there too, but the high number of customers is almost always based on passing trade that a more secluded restaurant must win over with other marketing.
2. The second rule is to find a restaurant full of local people and nothing too elegant. Furthermore, if the restaurant is full but looking from the outside you wouldn't probably have chosen it, then this is the perfect place to eat well!

Patience is needed:when you are travelling, the worst enemies are hunger and hurry, if you want to eat well. If you think that my approach is not that original you are probably also unconsciously using social proof.

In effect, every day we are victims of it, sometimes more, sometimes less. Near to where I live in Fuerteventura a really strange thing happens that borders on the paradox.

---

24. "We will use the actions of others to decide on proper behavior for ourselves, especially when we view those others as similar to ourselves."

On the waterfront that separates me from my daily lunch break there are two clubs "Los Pescaditos" and "Babel". Both are great local spots with good views and menus that are more or less the same.

As I pass in front of these local spots a lot, I noted a truly curious fact: one of the two is full with every table occupied whilst the other is almost empty.

The interesting thing is that the restaurant which is full is not always the same one :D

Sometimes it happens that Babel fills up first and othertimes it's its competition. People who pass by notice that both places would be good to stop and have a drink and decide exclusively on the basis of the people that are there.

If I was the owner of one of the local spots I would attract the first customers with a small gift to have some of the tables occupied. Social proof works, trust me!

Organise prices according to the rule of contrast

The last piece of advice based always on Cialdini's rule of contrast is to always place prices in decreasing order of scale from biggest to smallest. You can look at any of the tables that I have published up until now to realise that on the left I always place the higher amount.

The rule of contrast tells us that we instinctively tend to buy the things that we see in a successive order and as a consequence, the central price always seems more attractive to us if the price that came before was higher.

If, on the other hand you have to indicate the advantages in a list that can be read at a glance, I advise you to put them in increasing order for the same reason as I did for example, on the Reishi-Elisir page (Image 5.7). As you progress through the list, the product will seem more and more powerful and effective.

Image 5.7 - Use contrast to increase efficiency: the table is in increasing order (www.reishi-elisir.com)

Urgency and aversion to loss

Aversion to loss is a cognitive distortion that makes people more sensitive to possible loss in place of potential gain. The cause behind this way of thinking is easy to gather: in the older days to return from the hunt without prey was more acceptable than risking death on the job.

It is a natural mechanism and even the greatest predators tend to limit risks to a minimum and the probability of being injured during an attack. For example a shark rarely devours its prey alive, but takes quick bites to ensure that the prey has died bloody and defenceless.

5 – The rules of desire   169

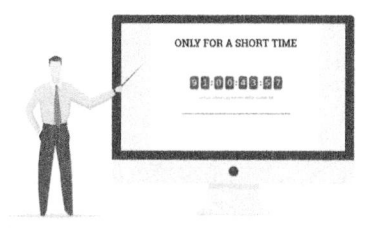

Using the aversion to loss means to induce within the people that visit our landing page a sense of urgency that they could miss out on the opportunity to take advantage of our offer if they do not act immediately.

It's a seemingly simple mechanism to use, so much so that even inexperienced copy writers exploit it often, but it's actually more complex than you might think and lends itself well to even creative uses. Remember that the human brain is designed to detect patterns: by identifying the model it's easy to unmask what are considered "trivial sales tricks".

Some proven methods that effectively exploit aversion to loss are:

A. Limited time offer;
B. Limited number of units available;
C. Limited number of units which can be bought.

> *Without a sense of urgency, desire loses value.*
> Jim Rohn

A. Time limited offer

The simplest and most widely used method of motivating users to buy a product immediately is to limit the time available. Some vendors use time-limited promotions where they discount their product by as much as 90%, but personally I think this approach is very dangerous. It's a forcing, and if copywriting isn't done perfectly, we may even run the risk of undermining the credibility of the entire offer.

"If the product really works, why would you discount it so much?" our user could ask themselves. The only credible motive to discount a product or service that much is for a pre-release announced while the product is still in development.

Perhaps after this book I will develop content to sell only to those who have already read this manual and the first edition of these eBooks could be discounted. Over time I could edit the contents again by adding examples, case studies and new tests. Whoever buys the first edition is very important to me because it supports my studies and offers me important feedback to improve my product. Making a pre-launch discount allows me to rebalance my relationship with my first readers but it should not be more than 30%.

The problem of the "super - non-repeatable - offers – but – only – for – a – short – time – so – act – quickly – or – die – in – misery" isn't only in copywriting. Nowadays, marketing is trendy and a lot of operators underestimate the importance of graphics and communication, creating web pages that are unashamedly commercial.

View one of their landing pages and you've viewed them all. The source does not reinforce the concepts expressed, the images are not exciting and the persuasive techniques used are often trivial transpositions of old models no longer effective.

You have to be different. You have to be unique and offer exclusive advantages.

As with consulting sometimes I do discounts but with a slightly different motivation. In the periods when I have a lot of work on but not many projects in the early phases, I discount my services around 20% to thank those who have had the patience to wait 3-4 weeks before starting the project. Entrepreneurs are often in a hurry but this is not always justified. Spending the right amount of time on each project, working with a calm mind and a tidy desk is of great value to me. The discount of 20% is

5 – The rules of desire 171

an amount that I am happy to offer to work well and start the project when my client has got all the necessary material prepared (I ask for the material during the initial stage at the moment when I accept the job).

To be able to visualise and make clearer the time limit on the offer you can also publish a countdown timer that reminds the user of the time that is lapsing until the end of the offer (Figure 5.8).

Conversation in English
Evening course worth € 549
in our headquarters in C.so Buenos Aires

30 hours in the classroom with a mother tongue teacher
15 meetings of 2 hours, once a week
with Final Certificate, after verification examination

Online platform
25 hours of access worth € 190
Comfortably from your home, whenever you want

Sophisticated online learning platform up to date (dedicated solely to company personnel)
The platform is complete with listening **comprehension** activities, videos, grammar, **productivity resources**, and much more

Limited Special Offer

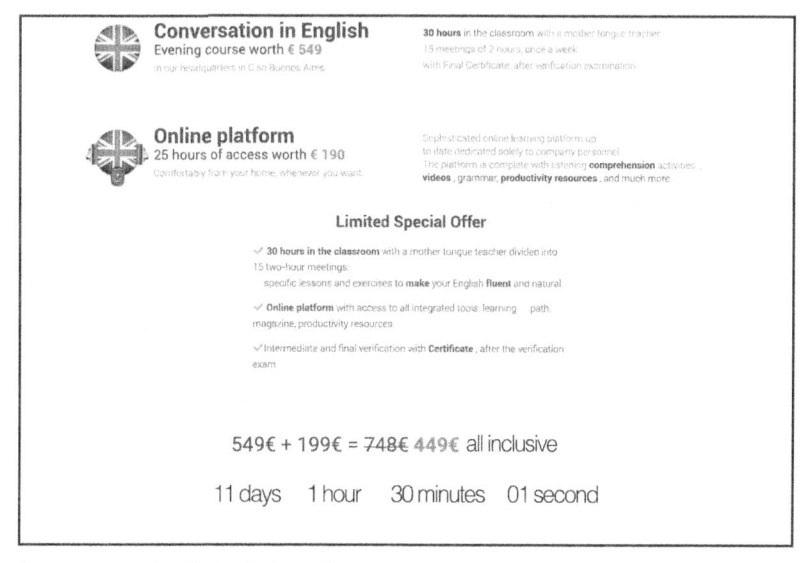

✓ **30 hours in the classroom** with a mother tongue teacher divided into 15 two-hour meetings:
specific lessons and exercises to **make** your English **fluent** and natural.

✓ **Online platform** with access to all integrated tools: learning path, magazine, productivity resources.

✓ Intermediate and final verification with **Certificate**, after the verification exam

549€ + 199€ = ~~748€~~ 449€ all inclusive

11 days   1 hour   30 minutes   01 second

Image 5.8 – The limited time offer and the countdown that persuades the user from losing the discount (www.conversazione-in-inglese.it)

The counter that I use is very flexible and allows me to set an expiration date and a text that appears during the countdown, as well as a text that eventually appears during the countup (after the offer has expired).

In this way the expiry of the offer is fixed, for example, 15th January 2022.
Other plug-ins have a customized expiration depending on the type of user who visits the page and make the countdown a certain number of

days and hours starting when the user visits the page for the first time.

This type of counter is very effective when used well (you visit the site and discover that the offer expires in 6 hours, 20 minutes and 8 seconds) to force the user to buy immediately but there is also a risk: when it develops through a cookie in the browser, if the user accesses with a different browser or with a mobile device then they could see that the counter starts from zero and then perceive this technique as too much directed at a sale. The risk as always is that the credibility of the offer may be minimised.

People who feel too forced complete resist purchasing, however, if we structure the process well we could even avoid this obstacle. The ideal is that the user lands on a page where they can see the final price or the price with a small discount. At this moment there are some users that will abandon the page, taking with them a small profile cookie.

On the second visit (about 30% of my visitors return to my landing page more than once) they will see the offer in a particularly advantageous way. Only at this moment do we show the countdown adjusted by a second cookie. The exceptional offer will then be shown when both cookies are in the device from which the website is visited and in this way the offer will be truly unique and directed at our user.

Thanks to this tactic we can take advantage once more of the anchor in the price, fixed in the mind of the user from the first visit to make them perceive the special offer as particularly favourable so as not to let it slip away.

An Invincible Offer.

ADVICE FROM THE AUTHOR

NEVER OFFER 30% FREE, OFFER 30% MORE

Another thing that you need to know about discounts is that to offer more products at the same price is a more effective strategy than offering a percentage of the same product for free, it seems the same, right? I know, but it's not like this. Even on this occasion, a small modification can make a big difference.

For this reason, years before soft drinks and detergents always had the same mark-up with a highlighted description on the label of 30% free whilst now, they use packaging which is a little bit bigger precisely to hold the part of the product that is free. If you think about the added costs of packaging a large distribution product you will soon be convinced that it must be really worth buying.

If you offer services, you could use this formula to sell your product at a price circling "giving away" an additional service. For example, if you are an author of a book about SEO and give courses about setting up businesses, you could launch a course giving away the book for free. The feeling is always the same: don't give a part of the product, but gift something else to the buyer, limiting the offer in time.

Presenting packs of related products is a very effective strategy as Amazon has experienced. If you try to get a copy of Influence by Robert Cialdini, the web will probably suggest that you buy this together with Contagious by Jonah Berger or Thinking, Fast and Slow by Daniel Kahneman.

The extraordinary thing is that buying in packs does not offer a discount and both books are sold at their full price, but even then people buy them in packs. The motivation can probably be linked to social proof (most people that have bought this book and also bought another) but also simple utility: when I have looked for books by American authors on copywriting, the system that Amazon has shown me about related publications has been very useful on many occasions.

B. Limit the number of available units

Another technique to exploit the aversion to loss is to indicate the remaining number of units to induce people to think that they could run out. Phrases like "last units available" or even better "last 3 units" is very effective in pushing people into buying.

This strategy not only motivates people into buying through the fear of losing, but can also be combined with social proof: we are naturally inclined to think that if a lot of people take advantage of the offer then it must be worth it.

Social proof is so strong that it can also divide opinions of people within the same group and even when it is a wrong opinion it can be very difficult to dismiss and can even activate areas of the brain dedicated to pain.

In one of the last episodes of "Brain Games" on the Discovery Channel, Jason Silva showed an experiment in which many people were lined up and in order had to give an opinion on a problem that was easy to solve. Everyone in the line expressed (voluntary) as part of the exercise a mistaken opinion and the last person, the subject being evaluated, had the option of saying the truth or adjusting to the group. Most people dictated an opinion consistent with that of the group even if they knew they were wrong.

If most people consider that the offer is amazing, we will also tend to judge it positively. We will not be totally dependent on the opinion, but we will be (to a greater or lesser degree) conditioned by it.

In this particular case the objective is to limit the number of units available, a strategy that I adopt on my pages. Beware though that it is not a matter of making artifices, but of writing effective texts that allow us to achieve the objective by putting us in a position of advantage over the competition (Image 5.9).

I have chosen to follow only three projects a month so that I can dedicate myself 100% to each project. This condition allows me to work well, but

5 – The rules of desire | 175

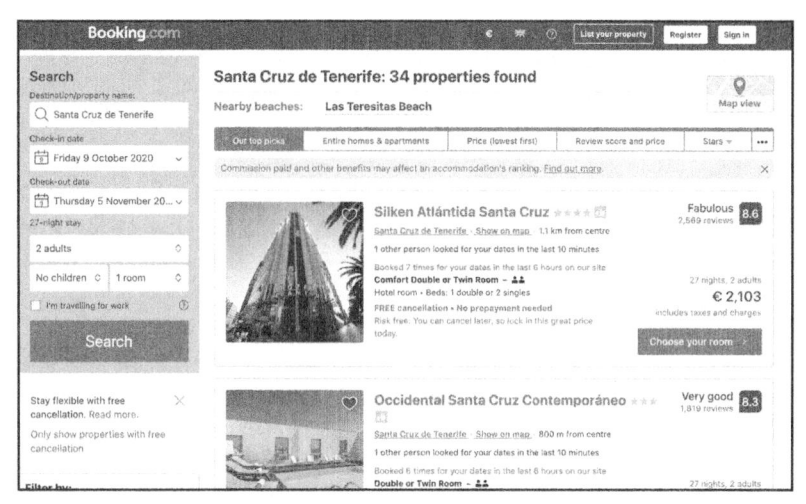

Image 5.9 – In their SERP, Booking shows the number of available places available or how long it has been since the last reservation was made, as if to say to you "Careful! You run the risk of losing the last room!" (www.booking.com).

often prevents me from following up on all the enquires that I received.

And on my page I mention it:

> "I will take care of your site personally, NOT STAFF.
> To guarantee the highest quality I only take on 3 projects per month.
> If you are really interested in finding clients online I advise you
> to contact me now so you don't have to wait"

I tell the truth and differ from my lower ranking competitors and I encourage anyone who is interested to contact me to do so immediately. I could have used stronger expressions like "losing the chance to work with me" but that would not be true and not credible either: if you have an interesting project, I will gladly work with you, at most, you will have to wait a little bit.

Being honest and credible is always the most important thing.

C. Limit the number of available units

It has been scientifically proven that putting rows of cans on a shelf with an inscription that says "you can buy a maximum of 5 units per person" increases the average number of cans purchased. Setting a limit has the effect of making an offer look particularly advantageous and indicating the maximum number of units that can be purchased sets an anchor that leads people to increase the number of units purchased.

Even a simple indication on a restaurant menu can contribute to a significant increase in revenue: it is enough, for example, to let people know that most people are satisfied by ordering 4 dishes. I have been living in Spain for some years and this indication is very useful for example, for all the tourists who have never had dinner or eaten tapas: knowing that a meal is composed of an average of 6 tapas allows an understanding of the average value of the bill and avoids customers having to ask the waiter for the size of the dishes.

This small modification is one of those that unexpectedly leads to big changes. What is really interesting is that it is relatively inexpensive to implement. All it needs is just a small label on the menu [19].

Desire after action

Four years ago, my landing pages faithfully followed the AIDA model and in my pages the wish area always preceded the action area, which concluded the page.

After a few months however I realised that the page presented a problem: it did not take into account all those users who, when they got to the form, were not yet prepared: some might need an alternative form of contact template, others might need information of an organisational nature whilst some wanted to know more about the company which developed the offer.

When a commercial offer is presented everything that has nothing to do with the product or increases its benefits is eliminated, but I have realized

---

19. Martin Steve J., Goldstein Noah J., Cialdini Robert B., The Small Big, Profile Books, 2015.

that, for some users, this information is important.
But this isn't all. In an article by Michael Aagaard I read that on a landing page for an Ebook, the references should be placed before and after the area dedicated to action, increased the conversion rate. I asked myself why. Probably what happens is that some users who are not completely convinced need some extra motivation.

So, a page that ends in the contact form will lack the following:

- Elements which calm those users who are still not convinced;
- Organisational information (why this offer was developed, who it's been issued by, which website the company is attached to etc);
- Last call, or a call to the action that allows the user to use an alternative contact form in case the main one is not to their liking (we may have provided them with a form and they prefer to call).

To these three elements however, I think there is still an element missing related to desire.

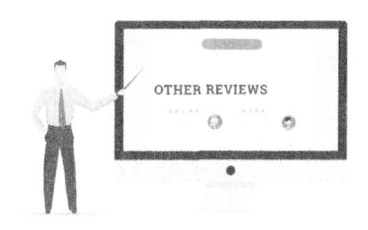

On my landing pages, after the box where I briefly say who I am and state the last events that I participated in as a speaker, I have published a video (Image 5.11) with a special script to push those users that are still indecisive to put themselves in contact with me.

This is what I say:
"Hello I introduce you Mark.

> Mark landed randomly on this page but he didn't know that to get results many skills are needed. Now he understands the importance of having efficent texts, awesome graphics and clear and clean layout, but he still has some doubts.
> He has read that taking an effective communication course would cost him at least 9000 dollars and even if he doesn't know how much a landing page costs yet, he still has some reserves.

The conversion phase

But, what would happen if he left the website now?

He would think that after all is not that important to have an effective landing page and without even realizing it, he would start to lose money every day.

What do I mean?

Let's immagine that Mark sells photovoltaic pannels at the value of 5000$ and his net worth is of 2000$. With the help of an effective landing page he could have 4/5 requests in a week and if only one of those would convert, he could earn up to 8000$ in a month.

How much does an effective landing page cost?

To find it out you can fill up the contact form. But I can tell you straight away how much it will cost if you don't get in touch with us. By developing an uneffective website to save a few 1000$ at the beginnig, Mark would risk later to lose up to 96000$ in a year. Do you want to divide it by 2 as yoou might think that I have exaggerated?

48000$ a year, do you still want to divide it by 2? As you might think that you won't be able to close more than one contract per month?

24000$ per year.
The highest cost of a communication tool is the one that you will pay by not using it.

These 48 clients could have made rich one of your competitors, making him stronger and more secure of his investment for the web site.

Call me now to get back all those clients who are going to your competitors and we will consider together if an effective landing page could be the solution for your business.

But attention, bare in mind that I only take on 4 projects in a month so call me straight away if you don't want to be put on a waiting list.

5 – The rules of desire

Thanks to this video I have the possibility to convince users that they have overcome the area dedicated to action once again fomenting the aversion to loss.

Right after this video I publish a small form where the user can download the quote by filling in only the name and email fields without the need to provide a phone number for the contact.

At the close of the page is the footer where I now present Futuraimmagine explaining that it is a web agency specialising in the development of effective websites etc. Only now, after the text, I publish a link that leads to Futuraimmagine.com where the user can find other non-specific references about landing pages which aim to testify to more than ten years' experience in web development.

Placing the area dedicated to action inside a sandwich that stimulates desire makes the page more effective. Some American-style landing pages continuously repeat the offer but personally I prefer a structure with a more ordered design where the user can orient himself more easily.

Image 5.11 – The video that exploits the aversion to loss presented on landing-page-efectiveness.com

ADVICE FROM THE AUTHOR

At this point at the end of each chapter I recommend that you take a break. If you have 15-20 minutes I suggest you go to the support page (https://landing-page-effectiveness.com/gym/) to put into practice the concepts set out and to better assimilate the information I have given you so far. All you will need is a simple sheet of paper, a black marker, a highlighter and a pen. With these exercises you can start to design your page, which you can develop as you read the book. Of course, it is not going to be the final one but it will be a great help to start translating these ideas into a design.

See you soon! https://landing-page-effectiveness.com/gym/

Chapter 6
THE RULES OF ACTION

> **What are we talking about here?**
> We have arrived at the conversion, our user have just clicked "send" on the contact form, however we ask ourselves, how much will their enquiry be worth? Are they really interested or is it just a waste of time? Is there a way to intervene in the types of leads that we receive? Is there something that we can do to facilitate the conversion action of our client?
> But, above all, once we have got their conversion, can we ask anything more of them?

As we have seen in the introduction, the landing page is one of the operational tools of direct marketing which by definition is always destined to make the recipient of the message perform an action. Our objective doesn't have anything to do with the reputation of the brand or the position of our product in the mind of the consumer: our objective is to generate sales.

By "sales" we mean requests for quotes, purchases, newsletter subscriptions or requests for information by phone, chat or instant messaging.

If in the first phase of the landing process the user was very close to a click to return to the search engine, now Google is a blurred, distant and unattractive memory. Whoever has delved into our offer up to this point hopefully must find the path to conversion smoothed out.

Before the contact area we must talk about a very important subject that

is often hidden on purpose by those who sell leads: lead optimisation.
Lead optimization & downsell

We have seen many techniques aimed at increasing the number of contacts that we receive from our landing page, but really, is this what we want? Do we want an infinite number of clients?

What is the real objective of a business that creates an Invincible offer? Collect all possible enquiries or generate profit?

The objective is to generate **the right amount of quality contacts**, optimising costs for the acquisition of profiled traffic, increasing the value of the acquired customer and making it profitable for the maximum time possible. As you have seen, I have specified several variables:

- the right number of leads;
- the right quality of leads.

We are used to hearing these concepts often in web marketing, but they rarely go deeper by defining the "right quality" and the "right quantity".

It's not written anywhere that a business needs an infinite number of contacts because their management has a cost and not every business has the budget for this: if I can start with only three projects per month, for me it would be useless to receive 30 enquiries per day. It would be better to obtain six but with a more suited profile, unless of course I decided to introduce into my business the sale of received contacts to my colleagues, converting myself into a hub /provider of leads. If the first objective is to generate the largest number of contacts possible, optimising conversions means going a step further, balancing the variables in play to increase the quality of the leads even at the cost of reducing their number to a manageable quantity.

6 – The rules of action

Obviously if your business is big and it consists of selling online products, it's easy to do the maths and keep the doors open but what would happen if you had a small restaurant on the beach with only ten tables? Would you really want to receive 200 email reservations per day at a cost of 3000 $ in traffic? Probably not. It would probably be better to receive 10 reservations a day investing 1000 $. But this isn't all. You would probably be more interested in filling your tables with mature couples that prefer to dine with a good bottle of wine, rather than adolescents that don't have much money to spend and ask for draft beer and something to pick at.

Just as a restaurant chooses the music and style best suited to its target audience, we can do the same on our landing page, introducing elements that "filter the contacts a little bit" to the extent that those that are only a little bit interested or not interested at all can be filtered away.

Here are some questions that might make you think about:

- The clause "satisfaction or refund" allows us to sell more, but, do you have to expose yourself to this small risk in order to get the desired number of customers or can you do without it?
- Adding online chat, for example, Zopim, which increases the possibilities of hiring also increases the number of clients who write without really being that interested just because it doesn't cost them anything. Is it worth it?
- Not indicating the price of the service will increase the number of quotation requests, but also the number of contacts from clients who are not willing to invest much and look for a solution within a low budget. Do you have time to manage them?
- Publishing an information request form with just a few fields allows you to get a lot more contacts, but if you get so many that you cannot manage them, is it not better to add strategic fields?

During the web Marketing Festival at the end of my presentation, one girl made precisely this observation: what is the suitable balance between quality and quantity? She had noticed that when she had reworked the form fields the number of contacts increased but that the quality of those contacts had decreased, so in the end she had decided to use a more detailed form.

The truth is that there is no single answer to this question and it is up to us in each case to evaluate the quality of the leads and to judge the balance of our landing page bearing in mind our time and our objectives.

The best way to proceed is always to approach it in layers, starting from the most complex (obtaining contacts), and gradually adding filters to increase the quality of the leads until you reach an adequate balance between quantity and quality.

For this reason, on my web pages I always publish the prices, I don't use an online chat facility like Zopim and I don't use a clause like "satisfaction or refund". Since I only have a few lines of development and deal with services (and not products) I can avoid doing this.

These tools work but even so I get more leads than I can manage and I often find myself having to give up projects, even interesting ones, due to lack of time.

Since I started writing the Invincible Offer things have changed a bit. If on the one hand, I could dedicate time only to people really interested in the development of an effective landing page, on the other hand I need to somehow keep track of whoever was interested in creating an Invincible offer. Some of the people who skip over the webpage don't have a profile suitable to the prices of the services, but at the same time they can be interested in the book and in creating an effective landing page by themselves.

If the page was originally supposed to filter out those who didn't have a budget (or weren't willing to invest in my service), now this group of users is interested again. I believe that this guide can be a great help for all these people, which is why I have done lead optimisation: I have done it in a way that a project to develop a landing page was always and immediately available to anyone who wrote to me or gave me his email, thanks to an auto-responder. This way, anyone interested in my service doesn't have to wait a second, finding my project immediately in their inbox. In this way I could avoid managing projects one by one and at the same time register all the email addresses of those that have put themselves in contact with me to let them know about the publication of this book.

Maybe you are one of these people! :)

When you ask too much: downsell

Since we created the Invincible offer, we had too many conversions and so we introduced filters to increase the quality, ok; but, what happens if the conversions don't arrive and the people who contact us are now too few?

Normally when this happens to me (because it does happen) I try and envisage the landing page from the outside with friends and colleagues and try to respond to the precise question: what is blocking the user?

Sometimes the obstacle could be that we are offering something that our users don't want or that we are asking for too much.

With a dental implant service, exactly this happened. My client, as a professional didn't want to give quotes online because they considered it unprofessional: how can you give a quote without first seeing the patient?

The objective of the landing page was to first obtain the appointment, free of charge at the studio. But very few people contacted the studio in relation to the volume of traffic, and I couldn't understand why so I did a search and I discovered that there are a lot of websites that offer online quotes for dental implants. Users want a quote, not an appointment. Now what? I thought. I was also supposed to offer a quote but my client didn't want to. No way. When you relate to professionals it is not easy to convince them of your ideas even when you are right, so imagine when you are wrong. And they were right, the online quote could not be given.

But we negotiated it and found a solution.

If people want a quote and we want to close an appointment, we can't let them get away and we must lower the value of the conversion to get their data otherwise they will be just ghosts.

I replaced all the "ask for a free quote" call to action with buttons that said "get a quote online" and the conversion rate actually increased because we aligned ourselves with the market demand.

But if we didn't want to offer a quote as I did? I used the auto-responder to say the same thing that is said to the person trying to get a quote over the phone:

> "In order to obtain a complete and precise estimate, a visit to the studio is indispensable. To provide a quote for a procedure as important as this without an appointment would be neither professional nor ethical.
>
> What we can tell you for the moment, however, is that the cost of the operations starts at xxxx Euros and varies according to the materials chosen. The average cost for an operation involving at least half of the teeth is yyyy Euros.
>
> In the next few days, Carla, our secretary, will contact you to arrange a free appointment during which we can define your precise budget with no obligation.
>
> Thank you for contacting us"".

Via this technique we could filter the users and obtain their details without violating the ethics that stop us giving a quote and at the same time having satisfied them, giving them the only thing that they really

wanted, which was a quote.
It's not our users that should adapt to us but we must accommodate them by trying to respond in the best possible way to their requests.

Lowering the level of the enquiry to obtain a lower value conversion (because in any case it would be better for people to go to the studio than having to contact them to try to arrange an appointment) is called downselling and is exactly the opposite of the process we have seen in the first part of the chapter dedicated to lead optimisation.
Downsell, combined with lead optimisation allows us to increase the average quality of our contacts recovering those users who are less motivated and who could be included in a distinct sales channel (maybe in a mail nurturing cycle).

A user who is not sufficiently convinced to fill in the main form could go elsewhere on the page and find information that increases the value and credibility of our offer in the section "desire after action"; once he reaches the bottom of the page he will find a small form with which he can immediately get the information he wants by entering only name and email.

Compared to the initial request, this second request will seem less committed and as a consequence, the chances of the user agreeing to enter their email will be higher.

The principle of contrast finds a new and interesting application here. I believe that the objective to be achieved, through study and practice, is precisely this: to be able to creatively combine more or less known principles to improve the results of a marketing strategy.

Simplify and facilitate contact

One of the main problems of the person who studies a lot and specialises vertically in something is that in a year or so they go through a phase where they think they know everything. It's a strange situation in which you tend to reason and develop projects without thinking that it can go

The conversion phase

wrong.

The same thing happens when you wake up during the night to go to the bathroom, but you are on holiday. Instead of finding the door to your bathroom you crash directly into the wall.

The path that has worked so far in your usual environment has suddenly changed and you are forced to keep your eyes open to understand how you can best orientate yourself in the dark in an environment you don't know. First of all, you bring your hands forward to avoid hitting your face again and start exploring the new environment until you find your way.

The next day you wake up and the pain in your forehead reminds you that during the night something didn't go well so you get up and start to observe your place with new eyes trying to find traps and paths. What went wrong?

Suddenly you are more attentive and start to work it out. You look at a simple wardrobe, in a place that seemed trivial to you, and when you open it you find yourself in front of a fantastic and unknown world. Narnia, for example.

For a moment you visualise the horizon of this new environment which up until now had been unknown, feeling like you are catching your breath.

Take a step back and you're back in your comfort zone. You sit on the sofa, recover your breath, broken by emotion and you realise that next to that wardrobe there is another similar one. And next to this one, another wardrobe. And another. And another.

For a moment you are afraid, then curiosity wins and you run to the doors. You open them, stick your head inside and in a moment, you are in Wonderland. You would never have imagined it, this also looked like a common wardrobe.
When you take a step back you return to your environment and for the

first time you look around you. You see walls full of wardrobes that you hadn't seen before and you don't have the minimal idea of what you are going to do. You know that you would like to visit these places but you know that a lifetime is not enough to get to know a single kingdom in depth and you feel overwhelmed by a feeling of confusion.

Whilst you return to your favourite sofa thinking about what to do, one wardrobe door opens and a colleague steps out. He has the same passion for knowledge as you do and is also passionate about Tolkien's work, so you let him tell you about his journey, while you tell him about yours. Surely you can never have the same experience as him, but at the same time his story is fundamental because it allows you to have a general and unique overview of an unknown environment narrated by someone who has visited it in depth.

My work functions in exactly the same way: each wardrobe is a specialisation or discipline which can be more or less close to mine, related and influential.

If on the one hand it is important to keep up to date and improve my skills, on the other hand I would never be able to do everything myself because out of my 10 hour working day I can only dedicate 2 hours to training and growth.

For this reason it is essential to create good relationships with people who have the same passions so that you can share their ideas, points of view and training. Selecting these people well it is importantto determining your success: the time that you spend with them can be something which can help you grow or simply waste your time.

On her return from a trip "Wonder Ross" (Rossella Cenini) spoke to me about Donald Norman, advising me on his "vision" of design[27] in one of his speeches on TED. Normally I wouldn't have come to Norman because unlike other authors (such as Steve Krug[28]), he doesn't deal specifically with the web, but speaks on a more general level, giving you a vision of what the design should be.

---

27. Norman Donald A., The Design of Everyday Things, Giunti, 2014.
28. Krug Steve, Don't Make Me Think!: A Common Sense Approach to Web Usability, New Riders, 2005.

According to Norman, the main function of design is to make an object comfortable and easy to use. As an example of extraordinary design, Norman chooses a door, any door.

According to him, it is an extraordinary design object because any person, facing a door, knows instinctively how it works. Grab the handle and pull if he sees the hinges, or push, if he doesn't see them. You don't have to think about how it works because it doesn't make you feel stupid or useless, it goes unnoticed carrying out its function.

But designers often do not think with this objective and consider only the aesthetic factor: they design squeezers that cannot be used, revolving doors that trap you inside them and websites which make users feel useless when they should be serving them.

If an object makes someone feel inadequate, continues Norman, the problem hasn't to be searched in the person who is using the object, as usually happens, but in that one who has projected it badly.

With websites exactly the same has been happening since 2000. The infinite creative possibilities of Macromedia Flash made improvised web designers generate monsters that are still struggling to survive in forgotten caves on the World Wide Web.

When an advertising graphic designer is guided in his work by his own creative inspiration and not by the communication needs of the project or by the ease of use, disasters occur in any field. It could be the interface of a web page, a revolving door in a public building or the logo of a business.

Beauty is incredibly overrated today. It is clearly an important characteristic for the success of a project but it is not the only thing that matters. It is not the only variable to take into account.

6 – The rules of action 191

When Flash started to progressively lose their share of the market until it had almost disappeared, we went back to a more content oriented website, but today HTML5 and CSS3 offer again creative possibilities that can put the self-esteem of the website users at risk and in the same way the sales of the website.

The priority of our website must be the achievement of the objective for which it has been designed. You must not create something incredible and memorable by its form, but by its content.

> *If you remember the shape of your spoon at lunch, it has to be the wrong shape. The spoon and the letter are tools; one to take food from the bowl, the other to take information off the page... When it is a good design, the reader has to feel comfortable because the letter is both banal and beautiful.*
> Adrian Frutiger

If you are a notary or a manager, your website should not say who you are, but rather sell what you do through a landing page capable of capturing a demand and offering the best response.

And most important of all, if you want to be contacted, are the methods of contact.

This is obvious, right? From what I have seen on the majority of web pages it wouldn't appear so. The fact is that it is not.

The most important element on the landing page is the one that should always be visible, at every moment and in every state and is not your logo, your header or your exclusive sales motivation, but rather the ways in which the user can contact you.

Perhaps they are already convinced that you are the best resource, because someone they value is already a client of yours and has told them the extraordinary things that you have done and they do not need to look any further but just make contact and talk with you. But on your website, you do not publish the telephone number. The contact page only shows the email address and you don't have chat. Your potential client, overwhelmed by all of these obstacles, goes to Google to contact one of your competitors.

Do you want to know what you can do to really facilitate the user's job on a landing page? Mainly, you can work on two factors:

- Make the contact form always visible (Image 6.1);
- Make the contact form easy to use.

These are some of the rules that I personally always use to be sure that I won't forget anything and so that other details that could be fundamental don't escape.

7 usability rules for contact forms

1. The telephone number should always be visible on every page, every screen and should be highlighted.

2. If you show the call to action on the menu, or a button dedicated to making contact, should be highlighted.

3. Even if you use a contact form specifically for receiving emails, you should always publish the email and the telephone on the footer. Even if you have already featured this elsewhere and publish your address without using fancy techniques to avoid spam

6 – The rules of action

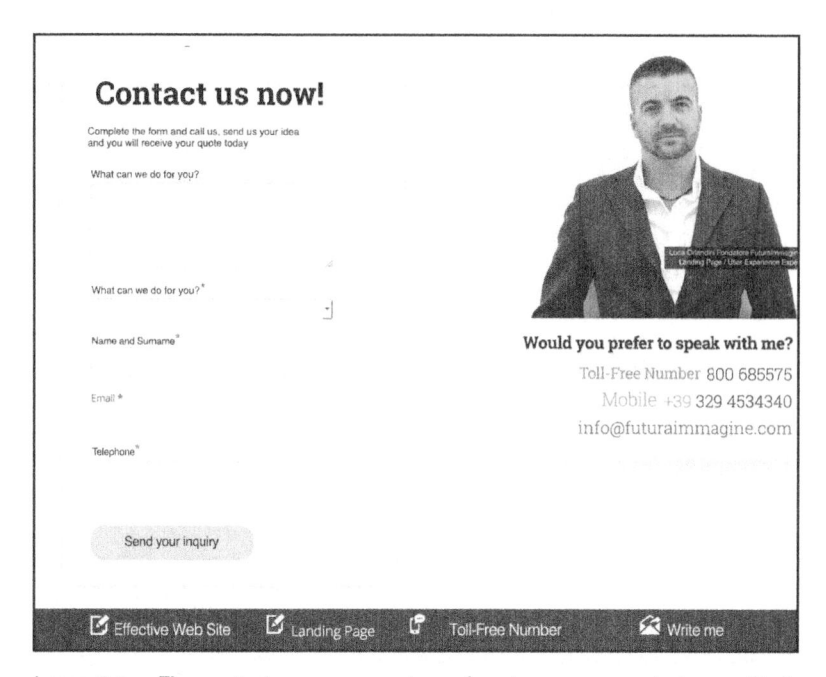

Image 6.1 – The contact area - present on almost every page. I always attach alternative contact forms to the public module. The dark bar which can be seen at the bottom of the page appears on every web version including the responsive version, where my personal contact via means of mobile telephone is published.

4. The telephone should be a link with a tag TEL: which allows the user to make a call with one click; the email should be linked with the tag MAILTO: which allows the user to send an immediate email. In Google Analytics these clicks should be counted as events which correspond to a conversion.

5. If you wish to monitor the actual number of calls received through the landing page, you can obtain a freephone number and publish it only on the offer page. Having a free phone number is a huge advantage to the client as you will always be available throughout your working day.

6. Next to the contact module, even if they are present and visible in other places, you should display the alternative contact details: landline number, mobile number, email and skype account..

7. Chats can further facilitate interaction with your users. Give it a chance and keep it if the quality of your contacts which it provides is good, in line with that which is explained in the section dedicated to lead optimisation.

7 usability rules for the contact form

1. Use a clear and clean design, I recommend that you put all the fields in a line, in one single column, one on top of the other.
2. Place the tags outside of the fields so that they will remain visible while the user is writing in the field.
3. In the beginning, if you want to improve the likelihood of the user completing the form, reduce the number of fields to the minimum. The aim of the module is to create a contact, not to thoroughly interview a potential client.
4. Use the system that highlights the required forms and which does not allow a form to be sent in which all fields have not been completed. Error messages often frustrate users.
5. Do not use CAPTCHA. The spam created by the robots outweighs any advantage. The modern systems which create more modern forms always use anti-spam systems which make CAPTCHA redundant.
6. Don't force the format. If a user has to provide a telephone number, do not try to control the format.
7. For the "send" button use a call to action which is coherent with the goal that the user wants to achieve, for example if the module has the aim of requesting a consultation, use "request your consultation now".

By using these simple rules, we can establish contact with the user. People particularly appreciate simple things and those which work well, and a clear and concise contact form will increase the credibility of our offer.
If our conversion plan is successful, at this point our user will carry out

the action for which the website has been designed and we will finally be able to say a toast to our first conversion.

But if we have finally reached our objective why are there so many pages left until we finish the book?

It's very easy. As foreseen at the start, the method TODAY the WINNER is YOU doesn't have just the simple conversion as its objective but aims at customer satisfaction and the creation of a lasting relationship on which successive sales are built.

And to be honest our landing page isn't finished yet!

The moment when our user decides to believe in us is when they clicking on the button to send the contact module corresponds to the moment when they most believe in the value of our offer: this is the moment to ask for more through an upsell.

Get more! Upsell!

The relationship between your effective landing page and your user is marked by a continuous oscillation of confidence.

We have managed to get them to trust us on many occasions and if they have performed the conversion action then we have done a good job of taking care of them without disappointing their expectations. They were hesitant and we have reassured them. They were wary of trusting us and we have given them guarantees. They were afraid of a high price and we have captured them with an irresistible offer. Now they have performed the conversion action and if the relationship with us has just begun, the one with our landing page has just ended. There will be other offers, other sales, but the web tour has ended exactly as we had planned. If our landing page had a smoking habit, this would be the time for a cigarette.

A lot of webmasters underestimate this moment and its importance leaving the user of the page with a cold "thank you" written on the mirror and do not know that you can get more and advance a little more in the relationship and make the moment even more special.

The moment after the conversion action is the moment of maximum confidence. The users is convinced that we are the best course of action for them and now wait for our call or our email reply. If only twenty minutes before they were unsure, nowthey are certain of their choice.

Some studies about the psychology of behaviour state that if a person is disposed to betting a certain amount on the success of an uncertain event, at the moment immediately preceding the bet they will be even more certain of winning even if the conditions are the same as when they bet.

It is the principle of coherence that we have already used on our homepage because we know well that:

> *It's easier to resist at the start than at the end.*
> Leonardo Da Vinci

What would happen if instead of making a stupid request in the wrong time like many web pages do, the request was made at the right time, at the moment of maximum confidence? The user has just believed in you, it's time to ask them for max. Make them land on a page with a normal navigation, consistent with the design he has seen so far, and start with a nice message of thanks to express your gratitude.

Then go to upsell asking for something else.

Watch out: it is only one more possibility that we should take advantage of, so the importance should be given first to thanks and after to the eventual upsell that should be written in an elegant and never aggressive way.

The action you want to stimulate in the upsell must obviously be consistent with the one the user has just performed. If a user makes the conversion

6 – The rules of action

into the inquiry module of an effective landing page, it does not make much sense to offer them the acquisition of this book, perhaps with a discount because it contrasts with the service they have just requested.

In my case it could have possibly made sense to download a report titled "the five things that people selling economical landing pages don't want you to know".

My service is better and more complete and, in knowing what cheap landing pages lack, will reinforce the conviction to confirm my quote.

If on the other hand, the same user has just purchased a quick start template from my web page which permits them to create an effective landing page they could find the advice that I have given in this book extremely useful. In this case the magic word is coherence.

If you are successful with your request with upsell you may obtain:

- The subscription to your newsletter especially adapted to those who have made a conversion;
- The possibility of activating remarketing with special offers dedicated to those who have converted;
- The sharing of your most important page, the Invincible offer, on social networks;
- The user may opt for a superior package (thanks to a discount);
- The filling out of a short questionnaire in return for a gift;
- The purchase of similar products ("clients who purchased this item also got…").

Let's look at some examples.

Let us suppose that you are selling a subscription service of a newsletter and that your client has just invested 20 $ in your basic package compared to the 50 $ which is the cost of the premium package. If I were you at this moment, I would offer the chance to upgrade to the superior package for 15 $ by writing something along the lines of;

"Thank you for purchasing our basic package, we are sure that you will be satisfied!
To show our gratitude for your trust we want to offer you a unique opportunity. If you had thought about the 50 Euro package but had considered that the investment was a little too expensive, to be able to enjoy all of the advanced functions for a whole year, for the next 24 hours you will be able to upgrade to our superior plan for only 25 Euros. Isn't that amazing?

The majority of users have already decided to take advantage of this opportunity but you are obviously free to choose and, in any case, you will have our complete attention, full access to all basic services and also to 24-hour customer care.

But please don't spread the word. This is a one-time limited offer valid only for a few days.
Thank you".

You can sell more or maybe ask for a simple share.

According to Jonah Berger, author of the fascinating "Contagious", one of the triggers which persuades people to share information is social currency, a true and real social currency which people happily spend in order to improve the perception which others have of them. Here we can see how some of the principles of psychology may be applied to a simple donation in order to capitalise to the full on the contributions of each one of the donees.

Do you believe that world peace is vitally important and have just made a donation to WORLD PEACE? Immediately after your donation you will be far more inclined to share the page on social media than when you initially landed on the page (the principle of coherence) and, if you are like the majority of people, you will be even more inclined to sharing if the message that you see is something like: "we are all one the same and we have to look after each other. For this reason I (principle of social value) have just..."

6 – The rules of action 199

I would leave the end of the shared post like that, with ellipsis. Thanks to the title, which piques the curiosity, your friends will click on the news, they will see that you have just made a contribution and will be motivated to follow (principle of social proof). Furthermore, if there is an important objective and this can be reached thanks to your contribution, you could also take advantage of the bandwagon effect, a variation of the principle of social proof whereby as well as following the masses we have the desire to jump on the winner's chariot.

In the offers we receive there is a great deal of psychology, recognising and understanding the mechanisms which govern our decision making nowadays is fundamental in avoiding being instrumentalised by methods of communication: not everyone who wishes to influence you has a noble motive or uses a method like TODAY the WINNER is YOU, which is also based on your final satisfaction.
Returning to our example of the one in search of funding, think of a shared post on Facebook which appears on your stream with the phrase:

> "Luca Orlandini (friend) has decided to support World Peace. As have Sara Paolo, Francesca and 137 other Luca Orlandini's friends and who you probably know believe that we are all the same.
>
> Don't look the other way, do what your friends have done and together you can achieve incredible things".

I believe that the this would work very well and would not even be very difficult to implement. Anyway, the thing that I am trying to get across to you is this message: "Never underestimate the power of the principle of coherence... the thank you page can present you with the opportunity to get shares but also direct sales".

Often, after you have signed up for a webinar, the "thank you page" also asks if you wish to purchase additional educational material (normally in pdf, mind map and exercises) at a very low price. This is the moment of maximum trust, of maximum conviction. If you have decided to dedicate an hour of your working day to education then investing 7 $ in additional

information would never be seen as a problem.
You can also recognise these techniques yourself even in the offline world and in daily life: for example, a friend of mine who goes on cruises told me that he ALWAYS reserves his next cruise during the last few days of his current cruise while he is still on the ship, in order to benefit from large discounts and promotions.

You only have to keep your eyes open and have the ability to identify the technique and you will find tons of examples.

ADVICE FROM THE AUTHOR

At this point at the end of each chapter I recommend that you take a break. If you have 15-20 minutes I suggest you go to the support page (Https://landing-page-effectiveness.com/gym/) to put into practice the concepts set out and to better assimilate the information I have given you so far. All you will need is a simple sheet of paper, a black marker, a highlighter and a pen.
At the end of this part you should have finally arrived at your landing page project. Have you done your exercises at the end of this chapter? I hope so!

If you want to finish your landing page project or maybe review it, I look forward to hearing from you!
https://landing-page-effectiveness.com/gym/

Takeaway

The Conversion phase: the WINNER
In this phase we must motivate the user to convince them that they should put themselves in contact with us (or make a purchase) immediately. The aim is to create a contact of the highest possible quality in order to be able to build a relationship.ón.

❶ Forging trust

1. Show the clients' reviews in a way so that they can be seen at a glance without using carousels or slideshows. Use stars to give a quick overall idea of the opinion expressed in the review. It's fundamental to include a name, surname and a photograph of the reviewer in every review. It would also be ideal to include a video but this is not always possible. An ideal review would be one which begins with the doubts and queries that the subject had before getting in contact with you and ends with the final experience (positive), adding the fact that they would recommend your service and giving a precise reason (indicate which one). It is convenient not to use only positive reviews. Insert the regular ones among the best ones, more or less in the middle of the reviews block. Try to post as many reviews as you can because they are important to users. If there are a lot, you can create a page dedicated to them to make them appear with a button. It is useful whenever possible to publish a couple of comments after the action area.

2. The satisfaction or refund guarantee allows users to buy without any risk and for this reason is very effective. There are various levels for this type of guarantee, some (for certain types of sales) are even required by law (it is called the right of withdrawal). The important thing, at the moment we decide (or must) use a guarantee of this type, is to make the most of its power of persuasion. It should not be a hidden possibility but on the contrary, should be well publicised and promoted and should increase the credibility and perceived value of your product.

The conversion phase

3. The free trial is the last step dedicated to the creation of trust. Thanks to this clients can try the service or product and get excited about buying in the future due to the principle of coherency. Users can be allowed to test the product or service at no cost or by asking for credit card details, which will allow us to set up an automatic subscription at the end of the trial period. The time of insertion of the card details is the most critical and therefore we have to think about our objectives and when it could be more useful to introduce them: do we want more users or more customers? The answer, especially in the start-up phase of new businesses is not as obvious as it might seem.

❷ The rules of desire

1. The first thing we can do is exploit the anchorage and bait effect on prices. We have created a first anchorage at the end of the area of interest and here we find a first comparison. The aim is to limit the user's choice to three options, of which two are real and one has an unbalanced price which – by contrast – will favour the solution we really want to target. There are several techniques related to both the copy and the graphic elements used in the page, such as indicating in red that there are only few units left. The idea is always to make one option seem more convenient by making the others less interesting. When we choose we act out of exclusion and block ourselves from the idea of making a mistake. Also, the principle of social proof can help us: indicate the "best seller" option that will let our user know that he or she has chosen like the majority of people in their situation.

2. Scarcity and aversion to loss are the weapons we will use later to increase the perceived value of our offer and arouse desire. Scarcity means that we tend to wish for those things whose availability is limited, while the aversion to loss depends on our fear of making mistakes and letting a suitable offer slip through our fingers (but also of losing a benefit not yet acquired).

You can use the shortage by limiting the time of the offer, limiting the units available or limiting the units which can be purchased. It is a very strong "lever", you have probably heard about it and even experienced its effects. If you plan to give discounts, remember not to exaggerate (no more than 30%) and that people would rather receive something extra than pay less for something.

3. "Desire after action" is a text area that, like the others in this chapter, has the function of increasing desire and is found precisely after the area dedicated to the action or to the purchase. It is important, because not all our users will be willing to contact us and then we must try to convince the one who passes our finishing line and keeps running in search of information. The first bit information you find should be aimed at creating trust and desire. I recommend that 2-3 positive comments are published right after the form (which will present a common data that is then brilliantly transformed into a good reference), followed by trust elements and information about the company providing the service. If it could be useful to link the institutional website to show the strength of the company behind the offer, this is where we should do it. In this area I publish a line about me and my specialization and the dates of the last conferences at which I gave a presentation (with the videos if I can) and finally a line about Futuraimmagine.

❸ The rules of action

1. Lead optimisation is a very important activity and has the objective of optimising the quality of received contacts. If up until now we have done everything possible to convince our users that we are the best course of action for them, the moment has arrived to discard those who are not really interested or are not included in the target of our service. We can improve the quality of our leads asking for more information in the contact form, eliminating the forms of contact less committed to the user (such as online chat) or publishing the price of our service.

All the techniques we have seen so far are effective, but they have a cost that must be weighed at this stage.
The downsell works instead in the opposite direction. If, after having published the landing page, we realise that the contacts that arrive are not so numerous, we have to find out what obstacle prevents users from contacting us. One of the obstacles could be the fact of asking too much, or that our users do not want to get in touch, but simply to obtain information anonymously. In this case we can publish a simple box where, by entering the email, they will get the information they are looking for. This strategy of lowering the level of inquiries could be used in any case, even if the landing works at the end of the area dedicated to "desire after action". In this way we can exploit the technique of the "door in the face". We make a complex request (a form full of fields to fill in), so that when at the end of the page and after other elements of trust, we publish a simpler form, the user who wants information tends to fill it in with less resistance. This way we will have two different types of users, one of high quality and one of lower quality/motivation but which can nevertheless be included in a nurturing mail cycle (we will look at this later).

2. Make easy to fill the contact form: this is the reason most websites are created. You must make all forms of contact visible at all times, especially telephone and email, and make the form easy for your users to fill in. The website must, of course, be correctly displayed on all devices, including mobile phones. Do not use CAPTCHA, do not ask for too much information and try to get a good balance between the quality and quantity of the leads received by opting, at least at the beginning, for the last one.

3. Get more with upsell. One of the most important and often underestimated moments is the one following the conversion: the "thank you page". It is the moment of maximum confidence with which you can try to get something more from your user but many advertisers and web developers do not take advantage of this opportunity: big mistake!

6 – The rules of action

With a well-developed page, if you try to make the user perform an action consistent with what he has just done, you can gain:

- a subscription to your specific newsletter for those who have carried out a conversion;
- the possibility to activate remarketing with special offers, dedicated to those who have converted;
- the social network sharing of your most important product, the Unbeatable Offer;
- the user's move to a superior package (thanks to a discount);
- the creation of a short questionnaire in exchange for a gift;
- the purchase of similar products ("customers who bought this product also bought...")

PART 3

The Satisfaction Phase
YOU

*To be successful you must contribute to success:
the effort, care and love for your work will always come
back to you, but only on the condition that you manage
to transmit it in the best way.*

INTRODUCTION

The subtle difference between obtaining clients and creating a successful business

If you have made it up to here you probably already have the first ideas to develop your effective landing page.

Even if you have followed all my advice to the letter, at this point you will need to gain some experience before you start generating your first results. You have a tool that is almost ready, a loaded weapon and therefore I think it is important to help you not to use it against yourself.

Having the ability to convince people to do something by motivating them presupposes a certain level of ethics that draws a sharp line between persuasion and deception.

This line is called satisfaction.

The very moment a person puts his trust in you and gives you money to solve his problem, your solution must fulfil the promises you have made. The reason is much more concrete than karma and much less philosophical than professional ethics.

You have to keep your promises because it's good for your business.

As a copywriter, I love American-style telesales, such as that of the famous Miracle Blade knife, which we have already discussed. If I had to turn an effective landing page into a video, I probably couldn't do any better. But what if when I received the knives, I realised that they are the same as all the others? That not only do they not cut the mustard, but that they make it difficult for me to eat a simple steak? Probably, at the first opportunity I would tell someone about it and in a few years, everyone would assume that a lot of lies are told on TV, that things are not what they seem.

The motive is simple and has been identified and codified[30]: as a social species we have the tendency to share "useful" information that can help the lives of those that we are close to. Although we can forget about giving advice about a good petrol station, we will hardly avoid warning our friends if the station employee punctually makes a mistake when returning change or that they are left with one or two Euros of petrol.

Sooner or later, and however your landing page may turn out, working poorly leads to failure. Always.

The YOU phase has been designed for this reason with a precise objective: to remind you that your client and his satisfaction should always be at the centre of the sales funnel. An extended satisfaction which goes beyond what he could have expected at the time he signed the contract with you.

Remember that TODAY the WINNER is YOU is not only the name of the method, but also, the promise that you make to your client.

If you have kept your client in the centre, he will be aware of it and be willing to put in a good word for you, leave you a review and introduce you to friends and acquaintances, but not only that: if you have gone beyond his expectations he will be happy to do business with you again and buy products and services from you again.

Selling again will be easier because the foundation of trust will be much stronger than you can create on a landing page on your first visit. Probably, thanks to this privileged relationship of trust, you will also have the possibility to sell products and services of a higher range that you would not have been able to sell at the beginning.

In the last phase, before the end of our journey, we will concentrate on expanding our sales funnel. In addition to paid advertisements which allow us to have traffic profiled, we will add a strategy that will allow us to obtain traffic at a fixed cost (such as writing a content) and consequently

---

30. Berger Jonah, Contagious: Why Things Catch On, Simon & Schuster, 2013.

7— Introduction 211

reduce the acquisition costs. we will then talk about the importance of having a blog, of creating an ebook, and above all, of making it available to those who seek information in exchange for an email address.

On the other hand, on the opposite side of the funnel, we will manage all the leads obtained through downsell in the best way, that is to say those contacts that are not yet ready to buy but that can be trained and stimulated until they make their first purchase. Through follow up marketing systems we can create contact lists that if treated with love and care can become an extraordinary business tool.

But before you are able to do any of this, you should satisfy your clients by rising above all of their expectations. Now we are going to see how you can do this.

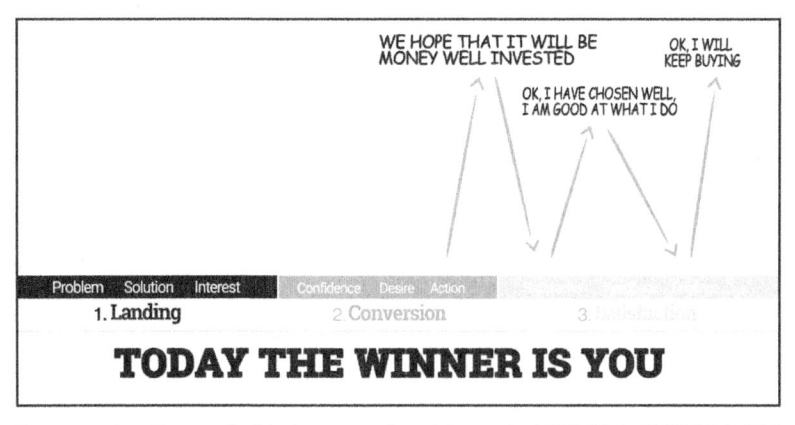

```
                    WE HOPE THAT IT WILL BE      OK, I WILL
                    MONEY WELL INVESTED          KEEP BUYING
                              OK, I HAVE CHOSEN WELL,
                              I AM GOOD AT WHAT I DO

  Problem  Solution  Interest   Confidence  Desire  Action
     1. Landing          2. Conversion           3.
           TODAY THE WINNER IS YOU
```

The conversion, illustrated with the perspective of the method, TODAY the WINNER is YOU

CHAPTER 7
EXTENDED SATISFACTION

What are we talking about here?
Do you remember in the first few pages when I spoke to you about "Scratch and Win"? When someone had bought a ticket and discovering he had not won, disappointed, he threw it in the bin? Our objective is exactly the opposite. With us you always win. You are a professional and I don't have to show you how to keep promises, but maybe you don't know the techniques that can optimise your efforts. If, for example, it has ever happened to you that you have dedicated yourself thoroughly to a project and felt that your efforts were not recognised, this chapter is dedicated to you.

We are facing the last test: if for many visionless marketers the game is already over (because we got the lead and then beat our competition), in my system we are in the second third of the process.

*Making promises and keeping them
is a great way to build a brand.*
Seth Godin

The satisfaction phase

Making promises is not enough. They have to be kept.

Actually, not. You have to go even further. Keeping promises is not enough, you have to give more. If you keep your promises, you will be at the right level, at the very least, of what your client expects from you. Keeping your promises means taking care of quality or providing a good service to your customers.

It's not cool. It's normal.

But our objective is not to put together a normal offer, we want to create an Invincible Offer, so we must be the best and go further. When I speak of "extended satisfaction", I don't just mean the way you have carried out your service or how your product has met the user's requirements.

I am talking about perception, but to make you understand what I want to say I have to tell you a story.

When I worked in marketing, I experienced a period of incredible professional growth that lasted about 2-3 years. I hardened as if I was in an iron-making oven, between stress and an amazing work rhythm but I was lucky enough to live that experience at the right time and in the right way, getting the best out of it. Other people who have travelled this same path remember with anger or discomfort situations that I remember with gratitude and esteem. The surprising thing is that the difference is not in the care or effort they put into the work or the result they achieved but in the communication with their superiors.

The most important thing that I learnt in this period was not the extraction of data in Excel, the organization of a contest for the sales network or the best way to promote a product.

I didn't learn a job, an occupation. I learnt to work.

7 – Extended satisfaction

In particular, the teachings that allowed me to survive and make the most of this experience were:

- The first was to not start doing anything without first **understanding** what to do, the priorities and the most effective way to achieve the goal. When you have a million things to do, it's easy to dive right in but it's easy to hit a wall and I couldn't afford to do it.
- The second lesson was to trasmit how every single task was important for me, even the tasks I was not able to carry out yet.

The exceptional vision of the person who had employed me was precisely this.

I remember that it didn't matter if I made mistakes, but on condition that those mistakes made me realise that I had made a mistake and above all how to prevent the problem from occurring again in the future.

ADVICE FROM THE AUTHOR

Don't be afraid to get it wrong
In Italy mistakes and failures are really frowned upon and the individual is often condemned for the same, and not his actions specifically, undermining his credibility.
In order to not make mistakes, entrepreneurs do not try out new ways of doing things and new ideas, but limit themselves to looking for something that works and that offers them security and then copy it and launch it on their small market. That's why I'm entrusted with clones of Amazon, copies of TripAdvisor and social networks such as Facebook. A lot of people follow only apparently marked paths to end up all in the same ravine.
Aspiring to success means taking into account the possibility of failure. Making mistakes is part of the job.

In my case the work itself was never that important compared to the possibility to grow and mature and to overcome and learn from mistakes and not make them anymore. In this way, a somewhat turbulent office, made up of people not prepared to carry out the tasks assigned to them became a perfect gear after three years.

The important thing for my boss was that we understood our mistakes. And some of my colleagues back then might laugh at this. We all make mistakes, and try to do our jobs better every day, but for my boss, the important thing is not to look for excuses but to understand why it happened. The difference between making excuses and explaining what happened was abysmal.

ABYSMAL.

We are talking about a half-hour telling-off with encouragement at the end to do better the next time, as opposed to three hours of beeing told-off with corporal punishment and final humiliation. Joking aside, it was the communication that marked the difference, not the quality of the work or the effort.

Everyone wants to do it well and they try hard, but do they really manage to convey it to their clients? The aim of this section is to pay attention to three fundamental points:

1.   You must always do a job that truly satisfies your clients, fulfilling the promises made at the time of sale. They must be aware of having made the right decisions and of not having made mistakes.
2.   You must go beyond the promises made, giving your client something that is not expected. Maybe something they needs, but at that moment they were not willing to pay (because of willingness or lack of budget). Something with a tangible and concrete value.
3.   You should avoid (and I know this is difficult) telling them that you have done more work and that it hasn't cost you anything. That it isn't important if it took you, say, 5 more minutes and that you would have done it for everyone else anyway.

The really strange thing that I have found in most of the businesses I have analysed is that almost everyone works like crazy to pursue the first two points, but almost no one thinks about point three. The enormous effort invested in the project is not even mentioned in a few simple words:

> "Don't worry, it won't have taken more than 20 minutes!"

> "It's no hassle, and it doesn't matter if it's late on a Sunday, I wasn't doing anything important!"

> "You don't owe me anything! Are you kidding! I was close by and it was no problem to come and see you!"

I know that we say these things to be friendly, but there is no point burning ourselves out if our efforts aren't recognised. We have eliminated the extra effort, like an eraser, for no reason whatsoever.

This is what Robert Cialdini spoke about recently in a live event, defining this type of person as a "bungler". If we do something for someone we should never underestimate the little credit we gain with our work. We always should give value to our time, our preparation and our ideas.

When I was going to business meetings with Pietro, the head of the advertising agency I worked with years ago, he often stepped on my foot under the table and gave me a dirty look during meetings with clients, because he claimed:
> "An idea that comes up suddenly and is thrown on the table during a meeting is not worth anything, even if it is good. An idea created in the agency and well organised is. Don't give away your ideas, sell them."

Whether it is sold or given away, the fruit of our reasoning always has a value, but if we are not able to recognise it, how can we expect anyone else to? The objective of doing something better is not to ask for more money, but rather to make our client see that we have taken this into account and that we have worked X hours that will not be billed, because we are committed to the success of the project.

I have done a lot of things for free but always with pleasure because they were important and I believed in the project. Because I decided that they were free and did not involve unforeseen costs: I have redesigned logos that would otherwise have made my work ineffective, I have created several variants of my landing pages, I have dealt with messy social profiles to create some order before launching pay-per-click campaigns.

I did it because I had to do it and because I wanted to do it well: the only communication that really works is the sincere, spontaneous type, which is born from a real interest in the project. You can't pretend, it's exhausting and it doesn't lead to anything good.

In this manual I don't teach you to sell just anything, but to extract and enhance intrinsic characteristics of your offer (or your way of working) that must be real. My work is to value them, but I can't create them.

These small details when they are correctly highlighted are decisive and so much so that they mark the difference between a relationship that continues and is enriched by new projects and one that closes by leaving things pending, even payments.

By adopting this philosophy, you can stop acting as a collector and worry about your bills being paid regularly. Customers tend to treat you with respect when they feel they are being treated equally, especially in an equal relationship of trust and respect.

Communication completely changes the rules of the game.

> "Do these last 30 changes or I won't pay you" is completely removed from "The programmer has worked an extra day to fix everything. It would have been 320 Euros but we'll give you a discount because it wasn't in the budget and it had to be done. I believed that to publish it online everything should be perfect..

The amount of work is the same. The result isn't.

When a person feels they have done a good deal, they are also willing

7 – Extended satisfaction 219

to speak of their experience, because of the already mentioned "social currency" effect. We are naturally inclined to share stories that make us feel better by choosing to be smarter and more savvy than other people. When we speak about these experiences, using words of praise for those who have treated us well, we use them precisely as if they were "social currency " through which we acquire the approval or positive judgment of our interlocutor.

By the same principle, whoever is satisfied with how you are proceeding, will be willing to speak well of you and leave you a review that will make your offer more credible and more effective.

> Word of mouth is the best medium of all[32]
> William Bernbach

As Bernbach argues in his famous quote, of all the media available on the market, spontaneous word of mouth is the most persuasive, as well as being the only one that cannot be simply bought with money.

You can only buy it with client satisfaction.

In the following chapter you are going to discover a scientific method to obtain the best reviews imaginable: an Offer, after all, cannot be Invincibile without them.

The satisfaction phase

ADVICE FROM THE AUTHOR

At this point, as at the end of every chapter, I recommend that you take a short break.
If you visit the website dedicated to the book you will find a simple exercise which will help you further understand the contents of the chapter which you have just read.

See you soon! https://landing-page-effectiveness.com/gym/

Chapter 8
OBTAINING REFERENCES

> **What are we talking about here?**
> In the chapter dedicated to trust you saw that reviews play a fundamental role in any landing page. I explained to you how to organise and customise them in the best way, but you still don't know how to collate them or how to make them persuasive and interesting for those who read them. I advise you follow this chapter carefully as it is one of the most important sections of the book.

One of the most powerful features of the system TODAY the WINNER is YOU is its ability to feed itself and to improve over time, adapting to the way users approach your offer, to make your landing page more and more effective and competitive.

In this section we will discover how to make our offer more credible and current thanks to the intelligent use of references.

Why will our offer be more credible?

Because the reviews are the only words that "haven't been written by us" and therefore constitute a fundamental point of view for those who do not know us. Constantly publishing new projects and references allows us to communicate love for our work and care for the satisfaction of our customers.

The satisfaction phase

Why should our offer be more current?

Because a person's fears and doubts can change over time and through references, we can also keep our offer updated with this important aspect in mind. The doubts that users had before carrying out the conversion action are a fundamental element of the reference and what makes the testimony more real and credible.

Asking for and obtaining references not only strengthens our offer but also allows us to impose ourselves on the market and obtain a good perception of the doubts and fears that we must overcome in order to sell.

Recent studies[33] have revealed that one of the key elements to success in anything is perseverance and effort... but we know that it is difficult to properly give 110% of yourself without motivation.

For this reason, reviews are such an important element that they are a considerable part of the payment, along with the money and the publication of the project in my portfolio: it is a fantastically vicious circle in which motivation is followed by more effort, more results and even more motivation.

Probably if I win the lottery tomorrow, I would continue doing my work exactly as I am today. For this reason, even though I collaborate every day with other professionals, I rarely accept collaborations with advertising agencies or web agencies: in most cases I cannot sign-up the projects in which I work or obtaining a review from the final client. If I discover some interesting technique, I will not be able to talk about it in a speech and a whole part of my life, as well as my experience, will be lost, like in the movie Paycheck. When I accept the assignment my customer knows that this clause has a cost equivalent to 30-40% of the value of the project.

If I had only developed projects in this way up to now, I would surely have had more money, but my landing page would have had no examples or references and I would not have been able to write this book. For this

---

33. Gladwell Malcolm, Outliers: The Story of Success, Little, Brown and Company, 2008.

8 – Obtaining references

reason, I advise you, always, no matter what work you do, to ask for references at the end of each project and to keep them carefully because when they are written in an effective way they have a concrete and quantifiable value that is maintained over time.

What am I referring to when I say "references written in an effective way?" I'll explain to you right now.

Effective reviews and useless reviews

Today everyone knows the importance of feedback but few know why it is so important and how to exploit it to the fullest. For this reason, this section is very important. The main mistakes made by websites in the review section in order of importance, are four:

- publishing false reviews;
- publishing real reviews but with little credibility;
- publishing real reviews but from an unidentified user;
- publishing real reviews but with empty content.

False reviews

A lot of web pages publish false reviews and in the Anglo-Saxon market there are even actors that record video-reviews for just a few $ (for example on Fiverr).

It has happened a lot of times to me that clients, maybe through laziness or testing me, have sent me photos and false reviews. I normally realise it between 4-10 seconds.

When you don't realise by yourself that the photo is a stock photo, you only have to drag it to Google Images to discover all the sites where it has been used. But it is easy to detect false reviews also because of the way they have been written: each of us has a different way of expressing ourselves and therefore I tend to almost never correct or reformulate the reviews I receive.

Real reviews with little credibility

One of the main obstacles that you have to overcome at the beginning is getting the consent of your client to use their photo. I know it's complicated and it also happened to me at the start, but it's fundamental.

An effective review is never signed by a business but by a real person. The photo has the important function of transforming an anonymous name and surname into a real person that whomever reads the review is able to identify with.

A good way of obtaining consent is to ask for the use of the photo that is already published on social media. Usually by making the petition in this way and explaining how important it is, it is rare for the person to refuse.

If you work with big structured businesses, the construction of the reciprocal relationship and above all upon which the reference is based, is generally more complicated, but in any way still possible. In addition to security and determination, a list of other large companies that have already contributed can be helpful here. Thus, taking advantage of the principle of social proof, you can increase your chances of success. If so many companies at its level have already done so, there is no reason not to accept.

From personal experience I can tell you that the biggest obstacle to obtaining references aren't the people that you ask, but your faith in the fact that these testimonials can radically change the value of your offer.

Real reviews but with which the user can't identify

A lot of business publish reviews without thinking about the fundamental characteristics that should constitute a review: the similarity between the person who reads the offer and the person speaking of their experience.

Social psychology studies have demonstrated that we are more likely to help and to believe in the words and advice of those who are more like us. The whole network marketing system is based on this fact.

As with the photos on our landing page, our user should recognise themselves as much as possible in the people who have chosen to use our product and who have left us a reference.

If, for example, in my project I have to promote a metabolic supplement that makes it easier for anyone to improve their appearance by controlling their weight, it is counterproductive to use comments from models or super sporty people. And vice versa, if my offer is aimed at sportsmen and women who want to improve their performance, I will only use people who are fit, or at least have a sporty appearance, in my references.

The reviews - as we will see shortly - are a means through which the target projects itself into its own future, identifying with those who have already accepted the offer and benefited from our product or service.

If it is not possible to feel identification the review will be much less effective.

Real reviews but empty of content

> "Of course! The reviews that are published are chosen by them and they are bound to all be positive."

How many times have you read reviews on a web page and thought this? A lot of people think that there should only be a 100% "positive" comments but this is not the main problem. Whoever published these reviews probably knew that client reviews are important, but because it's not real it's not truly persuasive.

The satisfaction phase

Like we were just saying, reviews allow our users to project themselves onto the future when they will have already resolved their need/problem that brought them to our offer.... but we must not forget that the moment that the offer is being communicated to them is in the present, and if they have not yet carried out the action of conversion, they probably still have doubts or fears to resolve.

Our real objective with the reviews is to bring any doubts and fears out into the open and then resolve them.

One review said:

> "With FuturaImmagine I found myself very pleased and satisfied with the professionalism and their availability. In particular, I had been very impressed with the ideas and the design of my landing page and with the effectiveness of the project that was developed".

Which is much less interesting for the user to read than the same review but with a more accurate premise:

> "I had had various bad experiences with webmasters who had ended up being basic executors of my ideas but by profession I am a dentist and not an expert in web marketing. Mr Orlandini has been unique in that he has been an integral part of the project working in collaboration.
> With FuturaImmagine I found myself very pleased and satisfied with the professionalism and their availability. In particular, I had been very impressed with the ideas and the design of my landing page and with the effectiveness of the project that was developed".

If a not completely positive feedback can improve the credibility of yours testimonials, it's above all in the possibility of feeling identification with any initial doubts that lies the secret for making reviews more interesting.

On my web pages via the use of analytical web tools, I have seen that users spend a lot of time on the reviews and the reading time isn't as reduced as consultants would want you to believe. Users look for information and they read it from beginning to end, especially when this information is clearly arranged and involves the user through a structure that reflects their emotional state.

You will have noticed that the experience told by Dr. Resta follows a structure that we have already seen: problem - agitation - solution. The review is real, but the way it has been structured is not the product of chance. Now we will see why.

How do we start?

If you have never asked for reviews before, let me advise you: at the beginning you will have some difficulties. I advise you to start immediately at the end of this chapter by drawing up a list of possible people to ask, starting with those closest to you.

Just like when you rehearsed the show in front of your parents as a child, it's good to start with the people you trust the most. The security and serenity with which you ask them together with the relationship you have built with your client, will determine the ease with which you can obtain them and will contribute to making you feel more secure in the future.

I started collecting reviews and using them on my website in 2004. One of the first ones was from my uncle, with whom I had done his web page, while another was from the head of the advertising agency with which I worked part-time. The third was from Paolo, a friend who had believed in me and Mambo (the predecessor of Joomla!), trusting me with the website of the company where I worked as a marketing manager. It is the trust of all of them that has allowed me to grow up until now: collecting these first references was much more complicated than it is now…but you have to start somewhere and then it's just a matter of not stopping and getting into a good habit by starting asking for references.

As your website fills up with references, you will find it easier to request them, and anyone who has to write something down will not feel the pressure of the blank page because they will be able to read and be inspired by the comments of other satisfied customers.

A good schema for making good questions to our customers come from "The Brain Audit", a wonderful book written by Sean D'Souza, one of the greatest marketers I have followed.

It's simple: good questions creates good reviews.

I know that it is strange but a lot of people have this problem: they want to leave a review because they are satisfied with the service, but it is simply that they don't know what to write because they've never done it for anybody before.

Between the different ways of constructing a credible review, I have discovered a very effective one that just requires the sending of a questionnaire that starts with a simple question[34]: "what was the biggest fear you had before trusting me with your project?" This approach soon revealed itself as the Holy Grail of references which, until then, had never been guided by anything that made them better or created a story with which the reader could identify.

Naturally, not everyone has doubts, or at least not everyone remembers them at the end of the project. Clients who come directly from being recommended by other clients, for example, often can't answer to this first question. So, I developed a solution. Although the problem is more effective because it solves a doubt, we can use a variant that allows us to use again the problem - agitation - solution structure[35]. "How did you feel before contacting me? What situation did you want to solve and improve once and for all? Why?" Also this question in substitution of the first one is effective too, because it allows our reader to put themselves in the skin of the one who already solved the problem.

Example of a doubt:

> "I had already worked with other consultants and other supposed gurus but they were all a waste of time and money. I have to admit that I was worried

---

34. D'Souza Sean, The Brain Audit: Why Customers Buy (And Why They Don't), Psychotactics, 2009.
35. Kennedy Dan S., The Ultimate Sales Letter: Attract New Customers. Boost Your Sales, Adams Media Corp, 2011.

about trusting in another consultant".
Example of problem /situation:

> "I had already worked with other consultants and supposed gurus but without success. I had to admit that I was very demotivated and almost convinced that my business wasn't suitable for the internet".

Regardless of the question, the result is similar and includes what would be the normal reference:
> "Ok, I'm sorry, I understand. But, how have you found it with us?".

The answer to this point will complete the previous thought, creating a persuasive story:

> "I have to say that with Luca, I found myself well looked-after from the very first moment and thereafter with the development of an effective landing page. He also provided me with new ideas for marketing communication that have proved to be very useful for the development of my business".

Or also:

> "I have never got on well in the water and I was sure that surfing wasn't the sport for me, but my friends insisted. Thanks to Stefano and Alessandro I discovered that I can surf with total confidence and I spent a really fun day with friends. I even managed to get up onto my feet a few times!"

Or even:

> "For days now I have suffered with molar pain but I was worried about going to a 24 hour dentist, because they usually cure the symptoms in a hurry but not the problem itself. When I discovered that the Abaco Studio could solve my problem definitively and at no additional cost I called them immediately and one hour afterwards I was well. Not only did I discover that the price was the same as the daily rate, but I also have scheduled the dental cleaning procedure that I had been delaying for lack of time. To be able to do this at night is ideal for people like myself that have complicated timetables".

By introducing the initial problem, like you can see, makes the review all the more real, because it goes further than something that simply says "well done, you worked well". In the same way, by publishing a review that is a little less positive, or even more detailed, you can contribute to making all the references more real and credible.

One of the most effective landing pages that I have developed for example, needed more than the usual 25-30 days to start getting results and although my client was very satisfied with the end result, in the review he highlighted it. I was happy to publish the review because it really expressed what can happen: even a specialist like me does not know how long should work to get results. It happens and the important thing is to always think, test and get the project off the ground.

When the same client, at the end of his comment, admits that he used to give only one course a month and that he now organises three thanks to my landing page, he immediately transforms a semi-positive comment into the best reference that can be obtained.

A good practice which I recommend is to always include, among the benefits of the service, the exact words expressed by satisfied customers in their references. By finding the same text at the end of the page, all your texts will seem more authentic and coherent.

Incredible, right? Through a simple process we can make our web page more and more effective and at the same time, know how to improve our service to make our communication more focused and coherent.

Let's start!

This chapter is very important. We have now put a little meat on the grill! Why don't we take a little break from reading and start now with YOUR review?
OK, try to think about the doubts that may have stopped you buying this book or if you didn't have any, about the situation you were in at the beginning before you knew the most effective method to create a landing page.

8 – Obtaining references

You now know how to identify the user's needs, how to choose images and text to attract their attention and manage it in the best way possible, how to make them interested and how to convince them to act immediately. We have also seen how it is very important to satisfy them and how to do it in a way that they truly appreciates our work… but try to go back to maybe the moment when you were in the bookshop or on Amazon when you asked yourself whether this could be the correct option for you.

Perhaps your web attracted someone once in a while but you felt that it could be working better. Maybe you just had a confusing idea of what a landing page should be and had to low your price to sell. Maybe you had already read something about social psychology but didn't really know how to apply it to your offer.

Think about it for a second and try to write the first thing that comes to your mind, in the most natural way possible. What doubt did you have about your purchase? Write it down on a piece of paper in a few simple words.

Now think about how many things we've seen together and tell me what you thought of this book so far, how you felt about the contents and even tell me which part you found more interesting and why. Be careful, you can choose only one topic, at most two. Being specific will in fact allow you to make your comment more useful to other users who are looking for information and want to get an idea.

Finally, if you want, send your review to feedback@landing-page-effectiveness.com and I will thank you by means of a surprise gift which will only be obtainable by users who send in their reviews and give me permission to publish them.

I will read all the reviews and tell you if they are structured in the most appropriate way.

It is also fundamental for me to receive your review. It is important for example to understand what content is most interesting and which direction to take to develop the posts on the help website. But there is more. Much more. I don't do training and I'm not a writer. During the day I continue to create landing pages for my clients and to write this book I had to give up going out with friends, gym and weekend breaks for about 6 months.

Knowing that I have been useful to you will be a great incentive to continue!

Thank you!

ADVICE FROM THE AUTHOR

At this point, as at the end of every chapter, I recommend that you take a short break. If you visit the website dedicated to the book you will find a simple exercise which will help you further understand the contents of the chapter which you have just read.

See you soon! https://landing-page-effectiveness.com/gym/

CHAPTER 9
MAKING THE FUNNEL EFFICIENT

> **What are we talking about here?**
> Your cuisine, right now, is based exclusively on high quality ingredients: you use paid PPC traffic, you discard of all the users who are not willing to buy on the first visit and you only offer your customers one sale. The funnel works, but the time has come to reduce waste and to expand the funnel from "simply effective" to "effective and efficient". A good chef will value the best ingredients, but he can also surprise you with a simple pasta with sauce.
> Let's start!

The last part of TODAY the WINNER is YOU is concerned with one important objective: the efficiency of our sales funnel.

If until now our objective has been to make the process effective (i.e. capable of producing sustainable sales) we can now think about how to reduce the acquisition costs and maximise the value of the contacts obtained.

Efficiency optimisations involve three main aspects: user acquisition, lead management and customer life-time value.

1. **Efficiency in the acquisition of users**
   Organic traffic from Google, which was initially not a priority, is beginning to prove useful, as it allows us to acquire users at a fixed cost (for example, by writing an article on our blog) and not at a variable cost (as in the case of the PPC). Creating qualified and vertical organic traffic on a problem is a rather complex operation that brings long-term results, but it will allow us to reduce average acquisition costs and therefore have a higher sales margin.
2. **Efficiency with the management of leads**
   The majority of people that visit a landing page do not convert immediately regardless of how much they are motivated by scarcity and urgency. Today we need to return several times to an offer before accepting it and therefore it becomes indispensable to "tie up" our users so that they never forget us. To do this we can use great tools such as remarketing and email follow-up.
3. **Efficiency of customer life time value**
   In a market where acquisition costs continue to rise, it is essential to implement a process that allows you to sell several times to the same customer in order to prosper. The system TODAY the WINNER is YOU is already orientated towards achieving this objective, because extended satisfaction at the start of the section YOU, allows you to create a relationship of trust which will facilitate successive sales. Have you thought of an upsell to propose to your customers satisfied with their first purchase?

As you can imagine, these activities are really important and they allows us to take maximum advantage of our work, but they are always subordinate to the process of acquisition and client satisfaction that we have already implemented.

Many entrepreneurs think they get results from the internet by buying SEO services to be more visible on Google, or they develop blogs to "stay in touch with their clients", but in reality they are light years away from creating an effective strategy because the lack of all the steps we have taken so far.

9 – Making the funnel efficient

The most important value that I want to transmit you is exactly this: the order of the activities upon which you should focus. The first that we have seen in the process TODAY the WINNER is YOU has been the search for the specific problem, do you remember? Let's see how this can help us create a blog and get profiled traffic at low cost.

Efficiency in the acquisition

Most companies use web tools as if they were analgesics: they invest time and money without asking themselves too many questions, hoping that the solution will come up by itself. But, unfortunately, it doesn't work that way. The task of an entrepreneur or consultant, even before knowing how to do something, is to know what to do and why.

This is how investments are agreed upon that are aimed only at advertising the brand or engaging in social networks, leaving aside the main objective, which should be the basis of each of our actions.

Does writing a lot allow you to position yourself on Google? Yes, it does.

Thanks to your company blog can you keep in touch with your customers? Yes, that's right.

Through "click-capture titles" you can bring Facebook users to your website? Great.

But if you don't sell then all of this is useless.

If your objective is to sell and therefore create a customer acquisition channel parallel to payment, you must have a concrete strategy. As Sun Tzu[36] used to say, victorious warriors first win and then go into battle, while defeated warriors first go into battle and then try to win.

---

36. Tzu Sun, Sun-Tzu: The Art of Warfare, Ballantine Books, 1993.

The satisfaction phase

In the development of your strategy it is essential to brush the dust off one of the sections of your landing page at the base of its own development: the specific problem of your users. Think about their problem and reduce it to useful content for your potential customer.

Think for example, of our Abaco Studio, which solves the problem of "after-hours" toothache with its emergency dental service. What could we write in a blog?

Personally, I would write a series of articles of the type like:

▶ "Toothache, the most effective pharmaceuticals to take away pain";
▶ "Toothache, natural remedies to reduce pain";
▶ "How do I sleep with toothache?"

And so. At the end of each article of course I would place a good call to action in which it would be read: "Have you tried these methods and still feel pain? Do you want to end the cause of the pain, at no extra cost? Come to the dental studio in Monza, we are open until midnight. Articles of this type, well positioned on Google, could bring to the dental studio users who initially did not want to go to the dentist, but were only looking for a method to relieve pain.

The only investment for this type of user acquisition is the time taken to write the blog articles and as you can imagine, over the long term this strategy if very advantageous because it allows us to intercept numerous clients at a fixed and non-variable cost as is the case with PPC. This content model is the most important and aims to generate conversions.
Other contents can be developed with the aim of improving the perception of the quality of the services offered in a specific field. Writing a technical article illustrating a new technique of implantology that provides the possibility to operate even on those patients with little bone tissue contributes to create in the reader the perception that the website that published the article is of a professional who is up to date and attentive to the updates in that particular sector.

In this case, the article could be published as a news item, but at the end

9 – Making the funnel efficient

of the informative part we can, in any case, insert a call to action aimed at sales: "Do you want a fixed prosthesis but your dentist has told you that you cannot because you have little bone tissue? Contact me or come to the studio, together we will evaluate if this new technique can be applied in your case".

The great advantage of creating a blog after I have developed the landing page is that I already have the editorial guidelines to create articles that allow me to convert users.

The landing page on Dr Resta's implantology site already presents the other two main advantages of his service which can easily be turned into effective content: "Do you want to switch to a fixed prosthesis but you are afraid it will hurt? Read the experiences of those who, like you, were afraid and decided to undergo the small operation".

In an article of this type we can focus on the fear of pain by explaining that dental implants, in modern implantology, are placed under local anaesthetic and that the discomfort is minimal: no marks or stitches. In the end we could say: "You would like to change to a fixed prosthesis, but you are worried about the discomfort of not having your teeth for days? Discover the advantages of an immediate load implant". The objective is to eliminate the fear of feeling uncomfortable during the period of time that goes from when the operation is performed to when the definitive prosthesis is fitted. With an immediate load implant, you can mount a prosthesis the same night of the operation.

Writing articles is easy if we have done our homework in the area dedicated to attraction. Articles are not more than tools to attract users in a different way who will then be directed to our sales page and through a coherent and progressive route, they will see that we are the best resource for their problem.

The "second" level of acquisition efficiency consists of the creation of e-books and downloadable content in exchange for a specific action that the user must comply with, such as sharing the resource on social networks or subscribing to a newsletter.

When I define the strategies for those clients whose contents I follow up, I start from here: I define a macro area of interest, I order 10-15 posts dedicated to a specific problem and then I collect them in an eBook that I make available on the website.

The articles are thus used at least twice: the first in the form of posts, which are published a week apart, over a period of a few months, and the second in the form of an eBook, which allows me to record the e-mail addresses of users interested in a specific problem.

Creating good content is important because when we know what content is useful to the user:

- You can write a post in a blog to share and spread on Facebook;
- You can film short videos to publish on a YouTube channel;
- You can summarise the contents in an infographic to put on Pinterest or Tumblr;
- You can group them all in an eBook to publish on your website and promote it on free resource websites.

In short, you can take your content, adapt it to different forms and promote it on different social networks. But all this work must be done to detect problems and then direct users who want more information to a direct contact or a vertical landing page.

Never, but never, should you write without objectives or with the wrong objectives, like, for example, cheating the search engines to obtain a better positioning. Your objective must be to satisfy your users, always and as much as possible.

There are no shortcuts to getting results, and our work must lead to slow but steady growth. If you think about it, we are not in a hurry because while we are implementing these processes we are, anyway, getting customers through advertising and our effective landing page.

If we work well, and aspire to be a good resource for our users, Google will realise this and sooner or later, we will be rewarded with lasting advantages, even in organic visibility.

Having a strategy will allow us to get more results and therefore dedicate more time to our content which dealing with a common and precise topic can be collected in specific eBooks like those that I have published for years in FuturaImmagine.

Why should you publish an Ebook? Soon we will see it in the next section.

Efficiency in the management of leads

One of the things that we have to fight against every day is the tendency of our users to not convert on their first visit returning to the web a lot and from different devices before converting and carrying out the action for which our landing page was designed.

How can we remain in contact with them? The main tools on which we can rely are two, remarketing and email marketing, and they use different methodologies to attract users and prevent them from forgetting about our offer.

How to get the maximum number of users with remarketing

Remarketing allows us to leave a file (called cookie) on the user's device, and then display specific advertising on Facebook or Google for a certain period of time before the cookie expires.

Have you ever visited a website and been literally "chased" by that brand's advertising for days while browsing? If the answer is yes, you have also been "victimized" by remarketing.

You can use this technique on a website through the Google Display network with Adwords or on Facebook, through Facebook Ads. Leaving aside the technical aspects, here too I would like to concentrate on strategy and content.

How you can pursue the user with a message consistent with their browsing experience?

Let's suppose that a user visits my website landing-page-effectiveness.com, but in the end decides to leave without contacting me and without downloading the project. I could make a message appear on Facebook that says something like: "If you know that most of the websites do not get results, are you sure you want to risk losing your investment?" I could do this message followed by banners or images extracted from the comments of my satisfied customers.

As you can see, if the objective of my landing page was to eliminate any doubt, now I must work on the contrary, to infuse the doubt of whether abandoning the offer was a wrong and dangerous decision for your business.

By clicking on the ad, the user could be directed back to my landing page or, even better, to another page that matches the ad they just clicked on. On this page I can delete the first profile cookie and place a second one with the aim of making him see a different and even more specific advertising.

Reducing friction and creating the most personalised route possible allows me to profile them better and increases the possibility of converting them into a clients. Pursuing users once they have left the website is a fundamental element to improve the efficiency of the sales funnel and reduce the costs of acquisition.

The second method to maintain contact with our leads is the most profitable and effective sales tool, the newsletter follow-up.

How to achieve conversions through lead nurturing

"Nourishing" customers through a follow-up newsletter is one of the

9 – Making the funnel efficient

most effective systems for generating conversions over time and together with an effective landing page, it is one of the fundamental assets of every company.

According to Google research, 91% of people spend quality time paying attention to their own emails every day and often even several times a day.

Our mailbox is a private environment that we like to go to and therefore we tend to give more trust to the offers that we like to receive and we consider those as an annoying violation the reception of spam and unwanted proposals.

I have placed the follow-up newsletter in this final part of the sales funnel not because it is less effective or important than a landing page, but only because a fundamental aspect of the process consists of an email address list, and to achieve this we need an opt-in page which must retrace the structure of our landing page.

An opt-in page has fewer entry barriers (the user must simply leave his email address and therefore the commitment on his part is minimal), but to convince him to sign up to our newsletter we must nonetheless capture his problem, shake it up, present our solutions, add elements of trust, create urgency and scarcity.

You have already heard of these things, right?

What is really important is that you have to erase from your mind the idea of being able to buy a database of addresses to which to send the newsletter. The address list is something that is created and cared for with time, like a small bonsai, but the results you can get from it are wonderful, especially when you implement your sales process on customer satisfaction.

I repeat the concept again, as it is the error into which 90% of entrepreneurs fall: the list must be yours. **Email addresses are not to be purchased**.

But, if you can't buy email, how do you get them? In the normal way: by investing work and effort in the correct direction.

The best technique is to create a free useful document for your users, making it available to anyone who agrees to leave their email address.

If you sell armored doors, for example, you could make a PDF like: "10 simple techniques to make your home safer". In the following newsletters you will offer free and practical advice to increase the safety of the readers' home, but also commercial offers that pursue the same objectives.

If you sell security systems and swimming pools you cannot send someone interested in armoured doors an offer on swimming pools, there would be no point. Nothing prevents you, however, from creating another newsletter list to send a PDF document with the title, "The expert's advice: clean a pool with 5 minutes a day".

Precise messages for precise users. Always.

Marketing automation systems can be used to create a follow-up, i.e. a chain of messages that are automatically and dynamically sent from the moment the user registers for the newsletter.

The content of the messages sent is generally of a formative nature and aims at gradually educating the users, who go from "cold" lead to an increasingly "hot" ones and are therefore ready to receive an offer that, sooner or later, will transform them into clients.

If nurturing our leads is important, we must never forget our clients.

With them, besides the marketing automation systems, we can also take advantage of good and old methods, such as the telephone, a personal email written once in a while (maybe to congratulate them, as Joe Girard taught), a message on WhatsApp or an unsolicited advice on something we have just discovered and experienced with effectively.

The key is to create genuine relationships and maintain them. When a relationship gets cold (even for natural reasons that has nothing to do with client satisfaction) a break-up can happen.

But we will speak about this in the next section dedicated to the optimisation of long-life customer value.

Increasing client life-time value

Consistency is really important and a lot of businesses have structured their entire marketing campaigns around this principle. As we do with our free ebook, these campaigns are based on the technique of "foot in the door" and on obtaining many small 'yes', in a progressive sequence of importance that ends with the purchase of the product, which allows the recovery of all costs incurred in the funnel.

An example of these campaigns is the fast food restaurants that offer fried chicken or hamburgers for a price that is almost below its production price to attract customers to the restaurant, sure that most people will also buy other products or in any case will come back later, generating the real gain.

Few large companies base their marketing on immediate returns, and most of them initiate processes that will prove to be effective and generate profits in years, not months, as, for example, the head of Amazon in Italy declared on Sky24 when it opened a few years ago.

The small and medium sized companies to which this book is addressed, reasons, however, in a different way and for experience, that it is best to see a quick return on its investment through fast and sustainable lead management systems from the start.

For this reason, I do not want to go into an analysis of this type of technique, but to focus on an aspect that is in any case relevant and fundamental: **you cannot base a business on a single sale.**

If the most efficient businesses are those that involve dependence (think, for example, of how coffee producers tie us to them through the capsule

The satisfaction phase

system), all efficient businesses must foresee several sales, generally of a progressive importance and value.

My effective landing page service, for example, does not include the operations contemplated in this chapter: there is a successive upsell, which is presented as a natural evolution of the project when my clients is satisfied and have recovered their initial investment.

Since I have kept my first promises and I have exceeded their expectations, there are no real reasons for refusing my next offer.

ADVICE FROM THE AUTHOR

At this point, as at the end of every chapter, I recommend that you take a short break.
If you visit the website dedicated to the book you will find a simple exercise which will help you further understand the contents of the chapter which you have just read.

See you soon! https://landing-page-effectiveness.com/gym/

Takeaway

The satisfaction phase: YOU
The time has come to satisfy users beyond their expectations, get feedback and motivate them to keep buying from us in the future by increasing the efficiency of our sales funnel.

❶ Extended satisfaction

1. To satisfy the users, give something extra. Now that our effective landing page has convinced the users to become our customers, we must keep our promises, going beyond their expectations. The best way to make them truly happy is to offer them something that they didn't expect and wasn't foreseen in the initial offer, as Seth Godin would say; a "fantastic surprise".

2. Value your gift and your effort. Something fundamental, however, is that beyond giving this gift, we must know how to give value to it, without underestimating our effort. We must differentiate ourselves, in practice, from those who Robert Cialdini defines as "bungler persuaders".

3. Show a sincere interest. A gift isn't an excuse to get credit and it should be a valuable thing. It is not fundamental and might not even always exist, but, if you can make that additional something else and give it to your client, the effect will be wonderful. Remember that the set must always be the result of a sincere interest.

❷ Get references

1. They should be real and true. Client reviews are a great tool to develop three fundamental functions: make the offer seem real, reduce doubts and stimulate desire. The majority of web pages however have a bad relationship with references, that are often false, lack credibility, useless for the user or unpersuasive.

2. Questions are fundamental. To get good references, at the moment of maximum client satisfaction, you can ask these questions in order: what fears did you have before entrusting me with the project? What stopped you from contacting me immediately? Would you recommend us to a friend or acquaintance? If the answer is yes, for what reason?

3. You should practise and believe in it. Gathering references is difficult, above all at the start but you should become used to asking for them. A reference stands the test of time more than a project and has a concrete value. It starts with the people closest to you, then gradually moves on to those furthest away. At first, feel satisfied with the ones you get, but never stop perfecting your reference portfolio, eliminating over time the less effective or representative ones in it.

❸ Making the funnel efficient

1. At the start of our sales funnel we have the sources of acquisition which for the time being are constituted only by acquiring potential clients. It is time to start attracting users also from organic sources, taking advantage of the tools that allow us to acquire with a fixed and not variable cost. We will be able to create a blog that takes advantage of the PAS structure (we identify a problem, we shake it up and we present the solution with a link to the landing), as well as collect similar articles in an eBook and give it for free to those who sign up for our newsletter.

2. At the end of our sales funnel we have a lot of users that have visited the page but have not realised the conversion action or have only left us their email in exchange for an eBook (don't worry, up until a certain point this is normal). We have to capitalise to the maximum the value of these micro results: we can recuperate the first due to remarketing (Facebook or Google), whilst the second aims to increase the newsletter follow-up. The majority of users don't convert immediately and return to the page to carry out the action: the more we manage to stimulate, the more efficient our funnel will be.

9 – Making the funnel efficient

3. After our first sale we shouldn't leave our relationship with the client to dry up. Effective marketing will always lead to successive sales with increasingly better value that aim to increase customer lifetime value. Creating a landing page to sell only one product is a great waste of resources, above all if our client is satisfied and would be interested in buying from us again.

FURTHER EXTRA INFORMATION

I hope that the journey so far has been interesting and that the end of this book does not mean the end of our journey of mutual learning.

I look forward to seeing you at the gym's web, which you already know about. Not only to go into the technical aspects in more depth, which in the printed version will become outdated very soon, but also to let you know about new techniques and get your feedback on the path we have walked together so far.

Thanks for your trust and see you soon,

Luca

FROM AN EFFECTIVE LANDING PAGE TO AN INVINCIBLE OFFER

An effective landing page is a great tool and is fundamental for the success of any business and I am sure that you are now convinced that: without an offer capable of converting users into clients most of your investments would be wasted and your business could be doomed to failure.

Now you have a clear method to formulate your offer and you are ready to launch yourself into the pool, but you still need to learn one very important rule before you start: knowledge of one tool, even if it is fundamental, is not enough to be sure of conquering the competition and the market. A more comprehensive plan is needed that includes an specific focus, which will result in a cohesive offer, and people interested in buying who will check out your offer.

To schematise, your business should have:

1. a brand positioning that takes the form of a specific offer, focussed on the needs of a specific market segment;
2. an effective landing page that offers the best response to a market demand, either implicit or explicit convincing users to act;
3. a source of profiled traffic that leads people to the offer who are potentially interested in buying the promoted product sooner or later.

These three elements provide the most important benchmark for your business, the one that will tell you how much success you will have in the marketplace. None of these elements (as in a multiplication) can have zero value, because it would completely cancel out the operation.

The value of each factor is not formed by a simple "true" or "false" variable, rather that each of the three conditions can and should be continuously **refined** to improve the total product of the formula.

If you thought you had solved all your problems with a landing page, I'm sorry but as I said it takes hours of work and several matches to get concrete results, but here is the good news: the reality is that there aren't many really competitive companies and most of them do not preside over specific niches, subconsciously allowing other players to conquer them.

A lot of web agencies don't have their own specific focus or a landing page to sell their own services, so it is hard to imagine how they would be able to communicate these important values to their clients.

"We develop your ideas and bring colour to your dreams", OK, but this won't make you sell.

The good news is that this situation represents a great advantage for us: obtaining results will be easier, because with our own merits we will be able to fill in the gaps of our competitors.

An investigation by E-Consultancy, for example, showed that in the United States for each 92 dollars spent to attract users to the website, only 1 dollar is invested in user experience and in the capacity of the website to generate conversions.

The advice that you have read in this book is unknown by the majority of people and the method TODAY the WINNER is YOU has only been published for the first time in this book. Keep in mind that, frequently, browsing between the offers of my competitors, I realised that the meaning of landing pages wasn't clear to them to the extent that sometimes it seems that landing pages are considered simple websites of just one page or squeeze pages useful only to register email addresses of visitors.

The second good piece of news is that in the next few pages we will go into more depth in the areas of profiled traffic and brand positioning so that you can have a basic knowledge also in these two disciplines.

Explaining it to you in depth during the course of this book would be impossible, entire works have been dedicated to it, but as I said at the beginning of the book, don't take it as written as verbatim that you have to do it all by yourself: what counts is that you have at least an idea of the situation and a basic understanding to distinguish a good professional from one who claims to be one but is not.

Targeted traffic

The importance of traffic profiling is easy to understand.

Imagine that you are a well-known chef and admired for your grilled meat. You work in a tourist town and when you do a barbeque everyone always leaves really content. Suddenly, the tourists stop appreciating your dishes. Following that, when you do your accounting at the end of the month you realise that 20% of what you have prepared, you have had to throw away. The following month it is 40% and thereafter 50% in the month after that. You doubt your ability, the quality of the raw materials and the taste of your meals. You ask for thinner cuts, you try to cook fewer fatty dishes and you change the recipes. Nothing. The truth is that you can't do anything other than look for work in another town.

The town you worked in, without you knowing it, has been advertised by chance on a vegan website, and thanks to its pristine beaches and low prices, it has won over influential people in the community. Due to word of mouth among friends and some comments on Facebook later, the clientele has changed rapidly, until it is made up of 50% of users of that particular website.

What I am trying to say, as you can probably guess, is that the quality of your product or service, or the way in which you present it, as effective as it may be, isn't sufficient to guarantee success.

It's fundamental that your offer is seen by people that are interested in buying because only with these potential customers will you be able to evaluate the capacity of your communication to attract and achieve results.

Fortunately, nowadays, having profiled traffic interested in buying is a possible and fast operation: you literally buy it from the person that sells it.

A PPC expert is able to optimize ads and destination pages to reduce your costs and select users within the target of your offer, identifying which of the two main platforms (Facebook and Google Ads) is the most suitable to capture your audience.

The importance of brand positioning

The importance of having a specific approach is however less evident to most. It has happened to me quite a few times in the past when I have asked entrepreneurs or sales managers about the target of their offer that I receive confusing and worrying answers.

In order to help you better, I propose a small test. See if you can answer the following questions:

▶ In developing your offer, have you done the impossible to satisfy the widest possible range of the market?
▶ Have you expanded the number of services or products until you are sure you can meet everyone's requirements?
▶ Have you ever managed, after a lot of effort, to develop an offer that had no particular drawbacks and was attractive to everyone?

Well done! If you have acted in this way then you have taken the path of

From effective landing page to an unbeatable offer

brand positioning in the wrong direction. Don't be surprised and don't worry, there are a lot of people in the market like yourself that a distracted observer might consider as well set business walking in the wrong direction.

But sales data tell us that this is not the case. In today's huge market, especially online, a wide range of products often means that companies have to measure themselves against the one thing that really sets them apart: price. We are well aware of how this type of battle ends. Margins that are reduced to the impossible and large groups that can make economies of scale, which are destroying the smaller ones after having weakened them for months.

Businesses that work nowadays are different and are characterised by a specific focus which make them ideal for one segments of the market, not all of it. In practice, by abandoning the idea of having to satisfy everyone will allow you to be truly appreciated by a more restricted public.

To explain what I want to say to you in a simple way, I must talk to you about Ana and her restaurant, La Arrocería.

Close your eyes and try to imagine that you are on holiday. You are on Fuerteventura, the beautiful Spanish island in the Atlantic and every night you have the opportunity to dine in a different restaurant. The local cuisine is really good and the unique geographical position of the island has allowed it to develop a very heterogeneous community where Spanish, Italians, English, South Americans and Indians compete for different tourists' tastes. The first night you walk along the promenade and you choose one of the typical local restaurants. The second and third night you try another two restaurants but on the fourth night you really want something unique.

You would like to eat paella since it is the first time that you are in Spain and you ask where. Everyone guarantees that paella is truly good everywhere but in "La Arroceria de Ana" they are real experts.

The only serve paella but it in a lot of very distinct ways.

You have been advised that you should book a table. In La Arroceria not only do they not have a person on the door inviting people in like you would find in other restaurants but the premises are often full. But this isn't everything. You find out that the restaurant isn't on the promenade where the rents are really high but it is in the town, 5 minutes away by taxi.

Everyone believes that a chef should be good at just cooking, but think how important it is to have a good marketing position. Ana managed to reduce the number of dishes on the menu, pay less for renting the premises, save the cost of having a person on the door and have the restaurant always full.

Ana's paella is fabulous but her success it not just down to her cooking. She is successful because she has chosen and managed to be specific.
A lot of people might think that not everyone likes paella, and that's true, but think of all the people who want paella and don't know where to go...

Ana (Image A1.1) suddenly becomes the only possible option.

Image A1.1 — Ana and her paella (I swear I was there!)

Your fantastic surprises

Different to a lot of consultants that try and dedicate a little bit to everything, for a while now I have decided to specialise myself in an activity other than branding or pay-per-click. Although as you might expect, knowing about these two activities is part of my job, there are vertical experts much more acquainted with the subjects than me.

My objective with this book was to communicate all of my experience in the process of developing a successful sale and I hope that you are truly satisfied with the content that I have shared with you as I have put all of my effort into this book.

But it's not enough.

As I have explained to you, it's important to offer someone that believes in us an unexpected gift, a surprise that can contribute to obtaining a common objective. Whilst I was writing the previous chapter, I couldn't stop thinking about you and it is time to give you a little present.

You should know that to make my projects more effective I use the experience and competence of two incredible teachers when I consider it necessary. Like me, they love their job, but they have chosen different disciplines. Disciplines that make them a real reference point for their market.

Without further ado, I have the pleasure, and am proud to introduce to you Marco de Veglia who deals with the extra information dedicated to branding and Rossella Cenini who will accompany us in the fantastic world of pay-per-click.

See you soon!

BRAND POSITIONING

Marco de Veglia is considered "the Godfather of brand positioning" in Italy.

He has in fact been busy with this material for almost thirty years as a consultant and represents the Italian office of the network Trout & Partners, headed by Jack Trout, the inventor of brand positioning alongside Al Ries[27].

He created the course, Easy Branding, the first and only course in the market that taught to create your own brand in an easy manner, via a step by step method. He has lived in many parts of the world but has worked principally for the Italian market and exclusively with 'Pymes'. He has left an indelible mark in the way a brand identity is built nowadays in Italy.

I am proud to leave him to speak and to thank him for this extraordinary contribution

Does a fundamental element exist for the success of businesses?

by Marco De Veglia

Now that you have learnt a truly unique method for developing a landing page… irresistible in fact. In this chapter you will discover one of two elements that, although "external" to the development of the landing, have an enormous influence on its results.

I want to talk to you about what I consider a fundamental element, common to all businesses that determines their success or failure.

---

27. Ries Al, Trout Jack, Positioning. The battle for your mind, McGraw-Hill Education, 2001.

Do you know what I am talking about?

I have been working with companies - of all sizes, from multinationals to small professionals - for 27 years now, and I can say that I have seen hundreds and hundreds of business situations. In spite of the variety of situations and jobs that I have carried out - in the company, as a consultant, as a service provider and even as a marketing director - I can calmly say that yes, there is a fundamental element, common to all businesses, that determines their success or failure.

I say fundamental because there are other accessory elements that contribute to success or failure and which must be taken into account, such as capital, production, sales and distribution, personnel and marketing and advertising activities.

But this is precisely the fundamental element. Or, if you prefer, it is the basis of your business. The problem is that in my experience most entrepreneurs ignore it.

Do you?

TEST: Does your business have a foundation?
Do this simple test responding to the questions below.

- Are you focussed on the clients and what they want?
- Do you believe that customer service and guidance are key to success?
- Is quality your strong point?
- Are you aiming for low prices? Or perhaps to offer a wide range?
- Do you think it is useful to have a creative and impacting advertising that makes people talk about it?
- Or, on the contrary, do you believe that marketing within your sector doesn't work?

If you have answered yes to the majority of all of these questions, I can tell you with certainty: like the majority of businesses, you have a business with no foundation or an extremely fragile foundation.

Brand positioning

The cement of a business is its brand. Or even better, brand positioning.

And if you answered "yes" to the previous questions, your business does not have an effective brand positioning. Or, more likely, it doesn't have one at all.

This is what I use for brand positioning

If you still have doubts that brand positioning is like the cement of a house, look at what happens if you do these things **but you don't have brand positioning:**

- If you have a great product, **it will be beaten by perhaps worse** products which know how to communicate a brand;
- If you want to do marketing activities…. **you don't know what to communicate and you'll throw money away**;
- If you have good distribution… it won't be for long because nobody buys your product;
- If you have good salespeople…. you have to resort to discounts, discounts, discounts!

None of these business activities – whichever type of business – is more important than brand positioning.

But…. the marketing? Isn't it sufficient to do marketing?

Of course, marketing is essential for whichever type of business.

But what is marketing?
I am going to give you a definition that will put everything into the correct perspective: marketing is the activities which makes you put brand positioning into practise.

Do you understand now how they work as a pair? In the rest of this chapter I will use the terms brand, brand positioning and branding in an interchangeable way, in no precise order.

The great misunderstanding of marketing in small businesses

I hope I have managed to explain how extremely dangerous it is for a company not to have brand positioning.

Unfortunately, it is not the exception, but the rule, particularly among small and medium sized businesses. For most small and medium sized companies, the brand concept is rather vague. It is seen as something for larger companies, large advertising budgets and television commercials.

"We are not FCA" is the concept that guides this reasoning. I have heard it many times. I'll explain to you not only why it is wrong but also why it is damaging your business.

If you are not big, you have to be precise

So, you are probably not FCA, you are a business, or perhaps a laboratory, maybe a web page or a professional and you are thinking: "Yes, a pretty argument… but, aren't these marketing things for big businesses with a big advertising budget?"

The answer is no.
It may seem paradoxical, and I may be the first to tell you this, but I have to tell you this: a big business with a big advertising budget can also have mediocre brand positioning and gets ahead thanks to distribution, advertising, maybe even the historical knowledge of the brand. But if you are a small company without resources you must have an effective brand positioning.
I'll explain why to you with a military metaphor that illustrates it well. If you're a big shot, you can afford to attack the enemy in the open, with shelling and thousands of soldiers shooting where they think the enemy is. Then, perhaps after millions of dollars wasted, you discover that where you have bombed and attacked was not the enemy. But, if you are a guerrilla and

you have only your rifle and some bullets, then you can't waste anything. You must become a sniper and aim carefully: every shot must be a hit.

In the war of marketing, the war of ideas and messages to occupy the mind of the potential client, you, like a small business, professional or commercial entity that has just started, you are a guerrilla. With little resources it is fundamental that you aim well. You can't shoot randomly. You have to aim like a sniper.

Your point of focus is brand positioning. So: **having a brand position is more important for a small and medium sized company** than for a large firm.

If you are convinced of this, in this chapter I will give you three key rules to create your brand positioning. I have summarised the process I am speaking about in greater depth in my course Easy Brand, the only course that exists in the market to teach brand positioning.

You can get to know the details of the course at: **www.branfacile.it**

But I believe that if you lend your attention to this chapter, you can obtain an advantage over 99% of your competition.

Rule #1 of brand positioning: "Use the stairs of the mind"

Where does marketing work? In shops, in advertising, in product packaging? Or maybe on the internet, Facebook and social networks? None of these.

Marketing does not work in supermarkets, in TV commercials, on billboards, in packaging, in public relations. Not even on the product. And not even online, not even on Facebook.
Marketing works in an ellipsoidal area of a few tens of square centimetres, not much bigger than a plate of soup.

Marketing works in the mind.

This is by far the most important concept to understand about marketing and brand positioning. The rest are operational details. Marketing works in the mind. In fact, it works on the mind. It works to influence it, to plagiarize it and to hypnotize it.

It is your current and potential customers' mind. It is no different from your mind, so you already have all the practical experience necessary to know how to work on the mind. Because yourself have been influenced by someone else's marketing.

Oh, I don't compromise, my decisions are always objective. Of course they are. Good marketing is not seen, it influences in such a way that it makes you believe that it is you who choose with your own motivations. But this is not the case.

The activity that develops marketing on the mind is called brand positioning. Positioning was invented by the aforementioned Al Ries and Jack Trout in the late sixties and is still to this day considered the fundamental key to marketing strategy.

What does it mean to position yourself?

The stairs of mind

Imagine that, for every category of article, there are stairs with three steps in your mind.

Choose a category that you are interested in and do this test: imagine stairs with three steps and now put brands on them. On the highest one put the first one that comes to mind and so on, going down. Consider only the first three brands (from the fourth onwards they count for practically nothing). Have you done it?

Maybe it was easy, maybe there were more than three brands and you had to choose. Or maybe there weren't even three, but only one or two. Or there were none, and this category of products is defined as "unbranded".

Think of cucumbers, coffins and beach balls (just to name the first things that come to mind). Zero brands, so you've invented a cucumber that doesn't go off when it's left too long in the fridge which can then occupy the "cucumbers" ladder with all the advantages that it brings.

Are you grateful for the idea of the cucumber? Why don't you like the Chiquita banana or the Marlene apple?

Because the objective of marketing is precisely this: to occupy the highest step on the stairs. The first, the leader, only has advantages.

The second is forced to pursue it, and the third must be consolidated with just the crumbs. And after the third one there are no more brands, there are only companies that try to survive by making discounts.

Therefore, the most effective positioning strategy is simple (not easy): it's to be the leader.

How to position yourself as leader

And what if the stairs of your category are already busy, which often happens? I will give you a good insight into the reality: if you compete in a local market or in a market with little marketing (many local markets, services or distribution, have little marketing) it is probable that the ladder of the mind for your category is empty.

But if you work in a category with a high marketing content, where there are competitors who arrived first...create another category and another ladder and place yourself on it as a leader.
And how can you create another category? It depends, objectively, on your market and the competition. But I can give you some practical tips that usually work:

- specialise: eliminate everything else and focus on the most important;
- verticalise: by target, by geographical location and by price;

- select distribution: a particular method;
- raise the price: it works if you choose to be "the most expensive".

Let's look at some examples:

- "specialists in home soundproofing";
- "commercial for the resale of cars";
- "home delivery only pizza";
- "personal trainer for VIP".

Be careful that you don't create irrelevant categories: "personal development for citizens of Rockport who are diabetic and fans of "Green Bay Packers" who play cards on Thursday night drinking Jack Daniels" is an irrelevant category.

Nice, but why do we need positioning?

I hoped you didn't ask this question, that the answer was already evident when we talked about the scales in mind. But I know that, actually, this question is the main reason why 99% of companies don't think about positioning.
Why do we need to do brand positioning? Because there are competitors.

And there you have it, if it weren't for competitors, everything would be much simpler. "This is my product, do this, buy it." There are however miscreants who may have come to the market before you or are bigger or better. Or, even inferior, but everyone knows them!

The problem that you have as an entrepreneur is that you don't have a market – and the mind of a potential client - virgin - in which you can say what you want, but must move in an already busy mind.

That is why you should use this model of reasoning which is the brand positioning.

That is why you should use the stairs of the mind. You can't see them, but they are there and they influence your success or your failure.

Rule #2 of brand positioning: "You should be different, not better"

"We are the best", "our product is the best" or – and this is really a classic – "we focus on quality", are the kiss of death for any business.

I beg your pardon!?

That's right, and I'll tell you why right now. There are two concepts that we must clarify:

- ▶ barriers to production (and quality) no longer exist;
- ▶ customers generally do not know how to objectively assess quality.

A new Callaway golf club, a leader in technology and innovation, can be copied by a factory in China in a matter of hours. Most industrial products can be reverse engineered and copied (perhaps even improved) in the Far East.
And if your business is not industrial, but maybe local or in a situation more complicated – for example, it is a service, it really is difficult for you to have any real and sustainable quality advantage.

But the problem is not even this: the problem is that clients are not able to objectively assess quality.

CLIENTS DON'T UNDERSTAND ANYTHING BUT THEY DO DICTATE

Excluding the industrial purchasing offices for a moment, if you sell to a consumer or even if you sell on B2B but the criteria of choice is not sufficiently measurable (as it happens in most of the cases), the client does not know how to value the quality and does not choose real quality.

He chooses the perceived quality, or a combination of emotional and rational factors that will tell him "this is a quality product". In the vast majority of cases it is the leading, or most expensive, or most rare.

Why?

Without going too much into the subject, this is how the human mind works. Since we cannot objectively go into all the problems that we have to solve on a daily basis, we tend to use substitutes, models that allow us to make decisions without too much information and reasoning.

Does a Mercedes cost more than a Fiat? It will be higher quality. Does a Rolex cost more than a Tissot? It will be higher quality. Do the vegetables from the greengrocer on the corner cost more than the ones in the supermarket? They will be better quality.

Clients look at other things to evaluate quality: if you are the leader (the first, the one that sells the most), if you cost too much, even if your product "weighs" more (in certain categories, obviously).

For this reason, it doesn't make sense to focus on quality, hoping that your client will choose you for quality. "Quality wins in the end" is the slogan of leading brands, those that sell regardless of quality and can therefore fool the competition by diverting their attention.

What should you do instead?

THE KEY STRATEGY OF BRAND POSITIONING: BE DIFFERENT

You have to be different.
You have to find something that differentiates you from your competitors and that this difference makes your offer more desirable.
The term "brand" is derived from the practise of marking cows in the United States. How can I distinguish my cow from your cow if they are the same breed?
Brand them in a different way.

How can we distinguish between two fish restaurants or between two

Brand positioning | 269

seemingly identical toner recycling businesses? One restaurant has its own fishing boat, the owner is a fisherman and the fish is, without doubt, fresh. A toner recycling business sells a subscription and regularly takes away old cartridges without you having to worry about it. These are two invented examples but I believe you have grasped the concept.

Using the idea of being different, moving away from the concept of quality and focus on your product, really makes the difference in your marketing and therefore in the success of your business.

WHAT IS THE BEST WAY TO BE DIFFERENT: BE A SPECIALIST

With this competitive concept, a specialist wins against a generalist, even if he apparently has to give up a part of the market. Red Bull basically sells only one thing: the energy drink Red Bull, and in 2010 it had an annual turnover of 5 billion dollars. The Coca-Cola Company has about 200 different brands with a turnover of $35 million. But with its biggest energy drink brand (Full Throttle) it doesn't reach 7% while Red Bull exceeds 42%. Red Bull, focusing on a single product, dominates more of the market than the other four biggest competitors (like, precisely, Coca-Cola and Pepsi).

Red Bull is clearly a hedgehog brand. Coca-Cola is a fox brand. Coca-Cola has hundreds of brands, but does not clearly focus on any one of them, as Red Bull does with its one product.

Red Bull is the specialist. In fact, it has invented a category, "energy drinks" in which it is the leader by excellence (see rule #1 of brand positioning).

BUT WE ARE SURE THAT THE SPECIALIST ALWAYS WINS?

Be careful: a lot of people notice that there are great brands that "do it all" (a typical example is Virgin, which does everything, and Richard Branson is always happy and smiling).

So, are there times when the concept of a specialist doesn't work?

This is not always so. There are two elements that allow big brands to be generalists as well.

The first element is that if a brand and a business are big, they are really big and they have enormous resources. If they compete in a lot of markets and are largely unsuccessful because they may be marginal, their survival is not at risk. And even less so if they are listed companies, where the logic of success or failure is more financial than market-related.

But you probably don't have these advantages because you are a small business. If anything, you may be interested in the second reason why a generalist sometimes seems to succeed. A generalist - in any case, a rather large company in its market - is successful until a specialist with enough marketing resources or a truly revolutionary product arrives.

If there aren't any competitors perhaps a generalist can do well. But when a specialist who knows how to do proper marketing and has resources to do it arrives, will inevitably conquer the market.

This has happened to various clients of mine, small and medium-sized businesses who decided to attack a market with maybe some big and old generalist operators who certainly had not positioned themselves.

With an aggressive positioning strategy on the part of my specialist, my clients have been able to conquer a portion of the market.

Rule #3 of brand positioning: "Always and only communicate your brand positioning"

Rule #3 is the easiest to understand and at the same time the most difficult to put into practise.

The reason is because of the very essence of being human, we don't get bored and we search for variety. And this also happens to businesses that in actual fact get bored of their own message and try to say other things as well.

A well-known story is that of Henry Ford, who, when he visited his advertising department at Ford, picked-up some advertising placements and said: "Is this it? It's good but everyone has seen it. Don't people want something new? What's new with us?"

The person responsible in the advertising department, clearly uncomfortable said: "But, Mr Ford, this publicity has not really come out yet!" Ford had seen it so many times in internal presentations that it seemed old.

But the fact of the matter is that, instead, to his potential clients, the advertising message, the characteristics of the offer and the brand promise were new. And the reason is that, in contrast to the person who is thinking 24/7 about their business, others have different things to think about.

And so? To do marketing is simple: always and only communicate your brand positioning. This is the simple but powerful secret of successful brands:

- They find a brand positioning that distinguishes the brand and makes it more desirable;
- they continually and always communicate it through all channels.

Therefore if you are a fish restaurant that has his own fishing boat (see the previous example) you should always communicate with messages like: "Fisherman's Restaurant. Here the fish is fresher because we catch it ourselves". And you will say this on the slogan, on the menu, on the posters, hear it on the radio stations, on the advertisements, on the brochures, on the direct marking, on Google Ads, on the Facebook page, on the emails and even on the local football team's shirts, if you sponsor them.

Shyness in marketing is a mortal sin. Say clearly why you are different, say it loudly, decisively, convincingly and repeat it.

Don't worry. You won't be monotonous. Or better said, you will, but it's what you have to do in a marketing message. People need to hear a promotional message a lot of times before it becomes their own.

"Redbull ..."

You will definitely have been able to complete the sentence with "gives you wiiings!" because this message is already in your mind and it seems logical. But before Redbull chose this brand positioning at the end of the nineties, nobody had this message in mind. After hundreds of millions and thousands of ads over the years, the message has caught on.

Maybe you are not Redbull and you don't have the money or reason to invest millions in TV (maybe you are a real estate in Holly Hills or a pub in New York or a surveyor in Louisville, or a company selling yachts costing upwards of 10 million. It doesn't matter: repeat your message with the means that are appropriate to your market and your means. And, I repeat, do not be shy!

To help you to communicate your brand message in an effective way, I want to give you a simple and efficient tool, which I always use with my clients: the brand positioning statement.

THE BRAND POSITIONING STATEMENT

The brand positioning statement, beyond the meaning of the English words, is a phrase that:

- exemplifies;
- explains;
- reminds;

your brand positioning.

It should not be creative, it is not a mission statement, vision statement or other abstruse term; it is a simple sentence - but specifically constructed - to guide your brand positioning communication.

The brand positioning statement has this format:

<brand name> is <what it is> that <distinctive characteristic>. Unlike the competitors who <do what the competitors do>, we <do what you do differently> and this offers the advantage.

I will give some examples (completely invented).

- **Restaurant with its own fishing boat**
  Fisherman's restaurant is a fish restaurant that owns its own boat.
  BPS: "Different to our competitors, that serve fish that they have bought, we only serve fish caught by ourselves and this offers us the advantage that we can guarantee the freshness and origen of our fish".
- **Hand-made linen-only tablecloths**
  Linen tablecloths is a brand of tablecloths hand-made exclusively from linen.
  BPS: "Different to our competitors, that produce tablecloths of various fabrics, we use exclusively only linen, which offers the advantage of indestructible tablecloths of the highest quality". which offers the advantage of indestructible tablecloths of the highest quality".

- **Indipendent Real Estate Agency**
  Your home is an independent estate agency that is not associated with any sort of network. **BPS:** "Different to our competitors that are associated with a network and are not located in city X, we only work in city X and we offer the advantage of knowing it better"
- **Web page that offers a dog training course**
  Meek dog is a dog training course that you can buy directly online.
  BPS: "Different to our competitors which require you to take your dog to a trainer, we offer you the method to train your dog at home with the advantage of being able to manage it better and save money".

I believe that you are have already understood how to use a brand positioning statement for your business. As you can see, it isn't a creative phase or advertising, but a guide for all the communication activities that you do, which also includes personal networking (especially if you are a professional).

When someone asks you "And what do you do?", you can reply "I am a consultant specialising in ETF.
Different to the majority of consultants that offer everything, I specialise in EFT because I offer my clients 2 fundamental advantages", in place of only "I am a financial consultant".

Is it clear how to use the brand positioning statement?

How to use the brand positioning on your landing pages

In this last part I will try to give you simple practical guidelines to link these concepts of brand positioning to what you have learned in this book.

I remind you of the three key rules:

1. Use the stairs of the mind, or find the way to be perceived as the leader of your category;
2. Communicate a difference in respect to the competition and eventually use the technique of the specialist;
3. Constantly communicate your brand positioning.

How to put into practice rule #1.

Find a way to communicate your leadership.

Personally, I believe that the use of #1 is always more effective (if you can say it). In fact, it cuts through the eyes and immediately communicates "leadership".

Generally, this concept won't be expressed in a heading, which you will reserve for the offer, but try to place it within one of the other elements on the landing page.

How you put into practice rule #2

The element of difference can be communicated on the landing page, or not.

Let's say that if it's part of the offer it's something great, but if you don't manage to place it then you'll have to communicate it in the next follow-up email. If you manage to insert it in the headline and perhaps even in the traffic-generating advertisement, it will undoubtedly increase the efficiency of all the communication.

How to put into practise rule #3

This, as we have said is simple: introduce possible elements 1 and 2 on your landing page to the maximum!

Last piece of advice

I end this chapter with an important piece of advice: brand positioning is often counter-intuitive, yet always rational. This means that you will encounter obstacles either within the company (employees) or in your own mind, which will make you question the decision and perhaps "try something else".

Brand positioning in addition has a quick effect and a slow effect.

You will see the quick effect from the start, when communicating your brand positioning you will notice that sales will be simpler and "natural".

The slow effect, however, is the one that focusses on making your brand work "on its own". There will come a day when potential customers will say "brand X is..." and they are speaking about your brand positioning.

At that point you will have really created a brand. But this takes time, because influencing minds with a new idea requires time "to settle in".

Build your brand. Everything else derives from this.
Marco De Veglia

TARGETED PROFILE

Rossella Cenini is one of the leading experts in Google Ads in Italy.

For the in-depth study dedicated to traffic I have requested his contribution because, compared to many Google consultants, she has a unique advantage: being a psychologist working in web marketing she has a different approach, based more on the knowledge of the decision making processes than on the simple - and perhaps more common - optimization of the technical tools.

If achieving a good level of quality and a low cost per click is important, I think it is even more important to understand users' intentions and what drives them to surf the web.

Thanking her for giving me the passion for cognitive psychology and for writing this extraordinary contribution, I pass the word to her.

Does a fundamental element exist for the success of businesses?
BY *Rossella Cenini*

In my previous life [...] I was a search advertising specialist. In practice I spent my working days trying to match traffic to client's objectives.

Many of the clients I had were convinced that it was enough to have traffic to sell. Of course, if no one visits your website or landing page, it is difficult to convert. This assumption, however, covers only part of the problem. We know that a conversion corresponds to the achievement of an objective on the web: sale, completion of a contact form, subscription to a newsletter etc, in short any action that has some value for us.

Well, then, the goal is to "increase conversions", but what are "conversions"?

Number of conversions =
Conversion rate x Number of Sessions (visits)

It follows that **in order to increase conversions, we need to increase the conversion rate or the number of sessions (or both)**. Obviously, we will not have to increase the traffic indiscriminately, but we will have to increase the traffic interested in our products or our services. The higher the initial motivation of the user, the easier it will be for us to "convert" him to the landing page.

In the Persuasion Slide™ model[38], Roger Dooley sees the conversion process as a slide, and one of the forces leading to conversion is gravity, i.e. the user's motivation. That's right, if we want our landing page to convert more users, we'll have to attract more motivated users to the top of the slide, then it's the Unbeatable Offer that will gently push them down (Image A1.2.1).

Before entering into traffic acquisition strategies, we must concentrate on our users and the phases they go through before reaching the "conversion" phase.

---

38. Dooley Roger, The Persuasion Slide, A New Way to Market to Your Customer's Conscious Needs and Unconscious Mind, Dooley Direct LLC, 2016.

The Persuasion Slide™

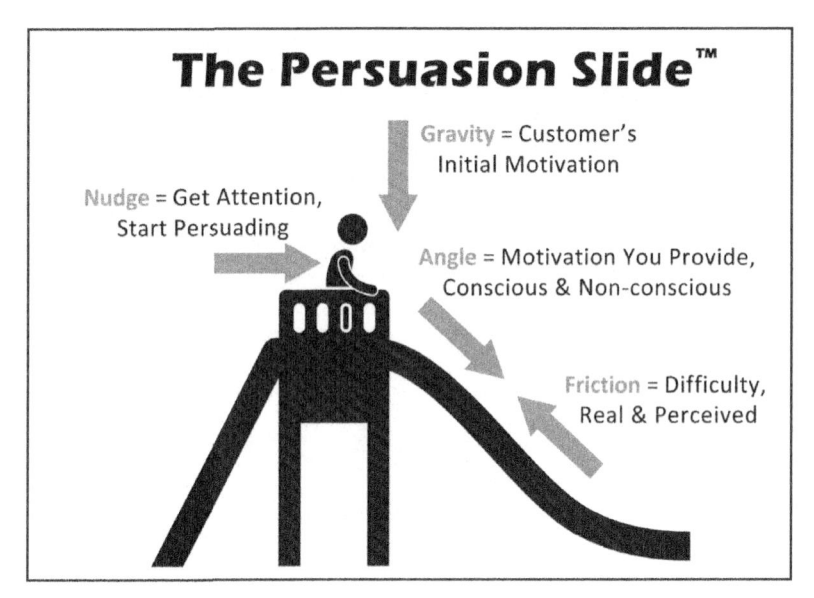

- Gravity = Customer's Initial Motivation
- Nudge = Get Attention, Start Persuading
- Angle = Motivation You Provide, Conscious & Non-conscious
- Friction = Difficulty, Real & Perceived

Image A1.2.1 – The persuasion slide by Roger Dooley.

The acquisition funnel: how people buy products and services

The process of making decisions consists of 5 phases:

1. **Knowledge.** If a user does not know that your product exists, he will never buy it (or even look for it).
2. **Interest.** Once users know about your product, you must create interest in the product itself. The user must think about your product and how it will "make his life better".
3. **Learning.** The user knows that you exist and is interested in your proposal, but needs more information to make a reasoned decision.
4. **Comparison.** The user already has all the information to be able to make a decision, but begins to compare with similar proposals.
5. **Acquisition.** Finally we arrive at the acquisition phase!

Extra information

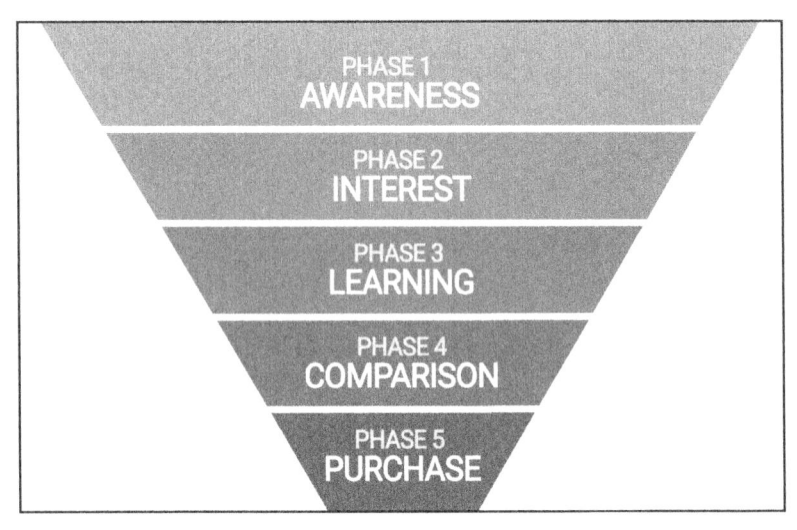

PHASE 1 AWARENESS
PHASE 2 INTEREST
PHASE 3 LEARNING
PHASE 4 COMPARISON
PHASE 5 PURCHASE

Image A1.2.2 – The acquisition decision process

As you may have imagined, it might be very difficult to reach users who are in the knowledge or interest phase with paid search engine campaigns only.

If users have a low knowledge of your product, they will hardly search for it in Google. You could try with the related searches, but you would run the risk of accumulating "expensive" traffic and above all, out of the target.

It's much easier with a search engine to capture users within the target when they are in the acquisition phase (they are looking for you and your product). For this reason it is very important to identify and define with precision our target audience: this allows us to identify the most appropriate channel to bring traffic to the landing page.

The knowledge phase doesn't only refer to the name of your product, but also to the problem /need. If a person has toothache at night time it is not fundamental that they know the name of a dental studio that is open 24 hours, but at least you should know that online you can find the solution to your problem.

Identify the target audience

Web page or landing page visitors can be divided schematically into three categories: those who will never convert, those who will convert anyway and in spite of everything, and "the undecided", that is, those who may or may not convert.

Our mission, if we want to bring qualified paying traffic, is to identify the undecided: then it will be our Unbeatable Offer that will convince them[39]. Correctly identifying one's own target audience is the first step towards creating successful campaigns. How is this done? We must ask ourselves a few questions. The answers will be the basis for our successful advertisements and for the choice of the most suitable channels.

1. **Who are our users? What blogs do they read? What pages do they visit? What do they look for in Google?**
   Let's suppose that we sell luxury shoes, like the ones adored by the protagonist in "Sex and the City". Your target audience will probably be (rich) women or lovers /husbands who want to give a gift to their partner. Of course, you can also do paid campaigns on LinkedIn, but will this be the best channel to capture your target? Before you say it: the rich woman could be a manager with an active profile on LinkedIn. Of course... but in this way you will only capture the socio-demographic aspect of your target, not all of their interests. She could be a high-ranking woman who only wears espadrilles because she is a fervent defender of animals and would never put dead animals on her feet.

2. **What is the main problem (or desire?) that our users want and can solve (or satisfy) with our product?**
   The answer allows us to identify the motivation that guides our users. Once you have identified "the problem" it will be easier to guide you to write ads that attract attention: you will make the user think "Hey, he's talking to me", and right after clicking on the ad he will enter a page that reinforces this conviction. On the other hand, you will manage to filter the traffic which does not have that problem, and which if it had

---

39. our task is ‚obviously, also bringing to our landing page whoever has already decided to buy. These are the easiest conversions. (AN)

reached the landing page would not have been converted.
3. **How do our users find information to resolve their problem?**
Answering this question will help you to identify the most suitable channels to bring willing traffic to you, as in the example of LinkedIn.
4. **How will your product make the life of the users better?**
Identifying this aspect is very important because it will help you write ads that are more focussed on the benefits being much more effective than those that highlight the characteristics.

5. **How is the user's decision-making process when he has to choose a product similar to ours? What are the doubts, hesitations and concerns of users when choosing a product like ours?**

You could, for example, add facilities to the ad to eliminate any possible reluctance from your audience by adding the "satisfied or reimbursed" clause or other element that reduces the perceived risk. Knowing our target audience therefore buys two invaluable aspects: it allows us to write ads that capture users willing to convert and allows us to choose the "highest performing" channels.

Google AdWords versus Facebook Ads

Google Ads (Image A1.2.3) and Facebook Ads (Image A1.2.4) are the two principal channels that allow us to attract profiled traffic (paid) to our web or landing page.

The substantial difference between the two channels is the search intention:

- The Google Ads adverts (either text ads or Google Shopping) have a clear search intention and search, expressed through the keyword used by the user.
- Facebook adverts (like companies Google Display or remarketing) don't have a search intention (they don't use key words) but their

Traffic profile | 283

RESULTS FOR GOOGLE SHOPPING FOR FUIJIFILM   sponsored

Fujifilm X-T1 Kit	Fuji X-T1 Black	Fujifilm X-T1	Fujifilm RR-90	Fujifilm X-T1 Kit
(XF 18-55mm	18-55mm XF ...	Mirrorless ...		(XF 18-135mm
1.099,54 €	1.259,00 €	764,99 €	36,62 €	1.290,53 €

Amazon - X Pro 1 Fujifilm -

Fujifilm "XT1"

Models: Xt10, X-30, XE2, XT1
Style: Reflex, Bridge

Image A.1.2.3 – Adverts from Google Ads. The user's intention is clear: find a Fujifilm X-T1 on offer. All we have to do is write an ad that matches the search intention and "combine" it with a landing page that is consistent with the intention and the ad. Only in this way will we be able to respond to the user's demand: the X-T1 on offer.

▶ advertising depends on other targeting criteria:

• Contextual targeting (Google Display Network): ads are shown based on the context of the page where they are inserted. If, for example, you sell cameras, you could post your ads on a photo blog. You may have seen banners offering cameras on photography blogs, or recipe book advertisements on blogs dedicated to cooking etc…
• User-based targeting: you can publish ads based on the user's interests and/or behaviour (this happens with Facebook Ads, Google Display Network and remarketing campaigns).

284 | Extra information

When a user searches in Google he has a specific objective in mind: to find the best answer to the question "expressed" with the search.

In remarketing campaigns the same thing happens, only the condition that determines the exit of the advertising is a previous visit to the website that publishes the ad. After browsing Amazon in search of a product, you may find the advertising of that same product on your Facebook wall. If with Google we must concentrate on the search intention, with Facebook we have to transfer our attention to our target audience and their interests. For this reason, Facebook is an optimal channel for generating knowledge and

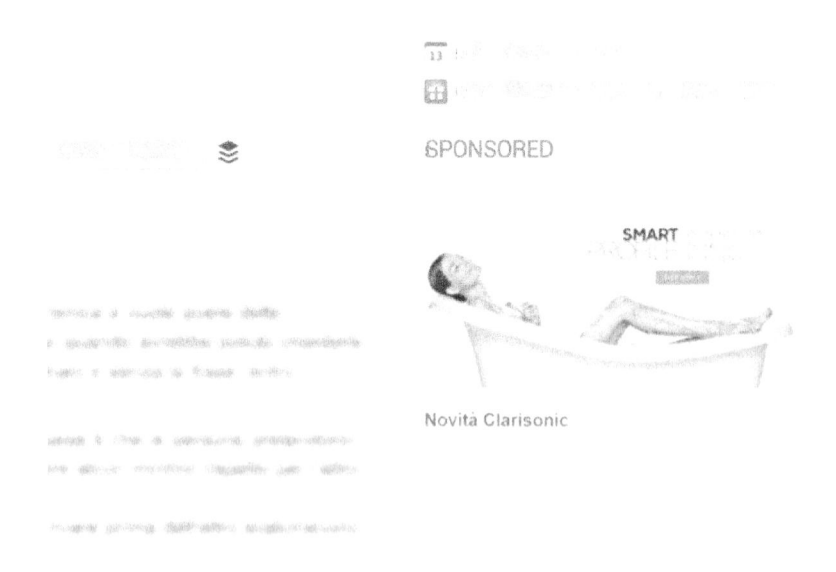

Image A1.2.4 - With Facebook, and display campaigns in general, things get complicated: users are not actively searching, but are busy looking at pictures of kittens. They're not looking for products (but might need them) and are seeing ads related to their interests and demographics.

interest, also taking into account that a Facebook browsing session is much longer than a Google search session (and that the costs of acquiring traffic on Facebook are much lower than those of Google Ads).

You will have understood that Google and Facebook target users who are in different phases of the acquisition cycle: with Google Ads (Search) it is easier to target users who are in the learning, comparison and purchase phases (Image A1.2.2), while Facebook Ads will be more useful in the knowledge and interest phases. The consequence will obviously be a different capacity for "immediate conversion".

Printed in Great Britain
by Amazon